Standing Still

Standing Still

SEEKING THE SACRED IN EVERYDAY LIFE

A Spiritual Memoir

Catherine A. Engel

Scripture passages, except where noted, are taken from the New Catholic Edition of the Holy Bible, 1957. Phillipp's Church Supplies, Fort Wayne, Indiana; Cleveland, Ohio.

ISBN: 1546501517
ISBN 13: 9781546501510
Library of Congress Control Number: 2017909086
CreateSpace Independent Publishing Platform
North Charleston, South Carolina

Dedication

This book is dedicated to my wonderful grandmother and mother, Alice Carney and Mineta Wise, who started me on my path to prayer, and to the "holy old ladies" of St. Andrew's Catholic Church, Abilene, Kansas, who inspired me to continue seeking holiness in my everyday life. My father, Henry Wise, while not a Catholic, taught me to value and respect the dignity of every person.

Acknowledgments

The old African proverb about its taking a village to raise a child is just as true when one is writing a book. There are so many people who encouraged me to write this one. Thanks to you all.

First, to my wonderful readers: Mickey Bogart, Norma Andersen, Karlin Gray, Anita Martinez, Lynne Barnes, Pat Kendall, Beth Elliott, Maria Fenty, and Father Teri Harroun: Your insights were invaluable.

To my indefatigable proofers and editors, Beth Elliott, Sanna Longden, and Pat Kendall.

To Dorit Knobel for her photograph of the Upper Room and Anita Martinez for the author photo. All the other photos used in the book are mine.

To Laurie Gudim for the realization of the cover.

To my outstanding massage therapist and good friend Maria Fenty for her willingness to discuss deep subjects ad infinitum. My shoulders and neck thank you immensely.

There were all the priests, nuns, and lay people who encouraged me to live a God-centered life: Msgr. C.J. Roche, Fr. Carl Kramer, Sister Redempta Eilert, C.S.J., Msgr. Bob Amundsen, Fr. Don Willette, Fr. Jim DeMuth, and Fr. Teri Harroun.

And lastly, to my husband, Pedro, for his constant support and love.

Table of Contents

	Acknowledgments	vii
	Introduction	xi
Part One	The Journey	1
Chapter 1	How Did I Get Here?	3
Chapter 2	Growing Up	9
Chapter 3	Learning to Stand	13
Chapter 4	Standing Up	20
Chapter 5	Standing in Trust	26
Chapter 6	Holding the Space	42
Chapter 7	Standing in Darkness	54
Chapter 8	Standing in Fear	75

Chapter 9 Standing on Holy Ground · · · 85

Chapter 10 Standing in Holiness · · · 116

Chapter 11 Standing in Integrity · · · 138

Chapter 12 Standing in the Presence of Mystery · · · 158

Chapter 13 Conclusion · · · 176

Part Two Resources for Entering the Stillness · · · 181

Resources for Entering the Stillness · · · 183

Bibliography · · · 207

About the Author · · · 211

Introduction

My impetus for writing this book came about one sunny Saturday afternoon during a wonderful sacred storytelling class given by Jane Anne Ferguson, an acting assistant pastor at Plymouth Congregational Church in Fort Collins, Colorado. Through Celtic folk tales and stories from the Bible, we participants were encouraged to dig into ourselves and to find our own deepest wisdom as to what each selection meant for us personally.

It was a graced day for me.

The final story Jane Anne told was the episode from the Gospel of Mark, chapter 10, in which Jesus heals the blind beggar Bartimaeus. Now Bartimaeus knows that Jesus is close to him because the noise and excitement is rising in the crowd. He knows that this is his one big chance to have Jesus restore his sight, so he begins to cry out in a loud voice, "Jesus of Nazareth, have pity on me!" The crowd tries to silence the beggar, but he knows what he wants from Jesus. So he keeps on trying to get Jesus' attention, crying out even louder than before.

Then Jesus stands still. He waits expectantly to see what will happen next, although it is pretty obvious by then what the blind man wants. After all, Jesus can probably hear the people shouting at Bartimaeus to hurry up, that the Lord has indicated He is willing and ready to see him. Nonetheless, Jesus does not hurry, He does not rush into trying to fix the man, He simply waits.

While some might say that of course Jesus knew exactly what He was going to do and therefore had no need to stand still, for me the fact that He did not rush into the situation says that there is power in holding back and not acting precipitously. He is showing us how to prepare ourselves for what is to come next.

In the end, of course, Jesus takes pity on the poor fellow and restores his sight.

Jesus stands still. There is power in standing still, and for most of us it is a difficult, if not impossible thing to do. Try it sometime and you will see what I mean. Whenever anyone says to me, "Stand still. Yeah, just like that. Don't move," I find that I immediately have an itch somewhere that must be scratched. First I begin to fidget, perhaps I feel a sneeze coming on, or some other physical problem asserts itself as being essential for me to take care of. Right now, this very minute. After ten or fifteen seconds I can't stand it any longer, and I begin to shuffle around nervously.

Stand still? Me? Hah! I don't think so. However, while obviously impossible for me to do, standing still apparently wasn't difficult at all for Jesus.

Another point I want to make is the importance of what Biblical translation we use. In all my years of listening to this story, I had never before heard the words, "Jesus stood still." In the Catholic lectionary that I am familiar with, the words are simply, "Jesus stopped." Because Jane Anne is a Protestant pastor, she was using the Revised Standard edition of the Bible, which Catholics almost never experience.

What a difference those few little words make! If someone stops, it simply means that they quit doing what they were doing before and do nothing else. Roget's *Thesaurus,* for example, uses as synonyms for "to stop" the words "to halt, to discontinue, to suspend, to put an end to, or to block." But to stand still implies waiting in expectation; there is a sense of awareness of the present moment, not just being idle. It is an active pause, not merely the cessation of activity.

I think the important part of the story is the idea that we don't always have to be in a hurry to get things done, although for most of us standing still and waiting is nearly impossible. We have become a culture of people who are *doers*, not *be-ers.*

And that is too bad. For while we are rushing around trying to accomplish this and that and everything else we neglect to be still and to see what our soul is asking us to be.

Because I have known since I was about three years old that my purpose in life is to be as close to God as I can be, that is my starting reference point in this book. Although many people use meditation as a way to get quiet, and that certainly is a valid reason for standing still, my main reason for writing this particular book is that the sacred can show up for us in any number of ways. Often times we don't recognize the holy when it comes, since it may be masquerading as something quite different.

Standing still can mean many things, among them the readiness to help someone else, or having someone's back. It may mean "to stand by" while someone else works out a problem. In that case, you are being asked only to wait and hold the space. It may mean that you need to take the time to slow down and meditate each day.

While I understand that meditating can be used to alleviate stress and to help us find better health, I have chosen to write about my own personal journey to God and spirituality, and that is the way I am thinking about meditation. I am using meditation and prayer as ways to find our own sense of wholeness and wellbeing as well as helping us to become holy people, so there will be a lot of discussion about God, in whatever way each of us sees Him/Her/It/Them. Since no one really knows what God calls Himself, we have to make up names that suit our own purposes. Therefore, I am going to be using a number of different terms, such as Yahweh, the Almighty, the Holy One, Source, the Mystery, as well as others throughout the course of the book. My own personal preference is to use the name God, or Yahweh, and the pronouns He/Him, but if you like a different name or gender, then substitute those.

There are many ways we can learn to be still and find out who we really are, and what Life may be asking us to do. The second part of the book has a selection of practices and resources, as well as definitions that I have found useful at different points in my own journey. Not everyone will be attracted to all the types of meditations, but that is all right. We don't all like hot fudge sundaes, after all. Some prefer apple pie, while others may elect to forgo sweets altogether. Pick and choose what feels right for you.

My background is thoroughly grounded in Roman Catholicism, as that is the church I was raised in. These days, however, I attend an Ecumenical Catholic Church instead, preferring the inclusivity and broader perspective that were espoused by that great saint, Pope John XXIII. But the Mass and the sacraments are the same in either case, as is the whole body of prayer practices.

I am making a point here about the types of exercises I have included, and why so many of them are from the Catholic perspective. Obviously, since Catholicism is the tradition I know best, many of the practices I include come from that background. However, there are some exercises based on Eastern philosophies as well.

Much of what I have learned over the years began as a search for physical healing, and I ended up in some very strange places as a result. I could never have imagined where this life would take me, but I am so grateful for the joy I have received as a result of that journey.

I would imagine that pretty much everyone who lives on this planet will find that the path they originally set out for themselves in their youth has taken some dramatic and sometimes unexpected twists and turns. There are bound to be setbacks in the form of lost friendships, new jobs, moves to a new city, marriage and sometimes divorce, not to mention illnesses and death. Throughout all of these meanderings, there will always be some sadness along with the excitement and joy of living, but one thing we can be sure of: There will also be gifts and blessings to help us along the way. We just have to learn how to be open to whatever shows up for us. God is always at work in us, but we have to be open to receive whatever that is. The form may be different from what we expect, or something entirely new may make us re-evaluate everything we thought we knew.

If we can just be willing to experience these new things, and if we can trust that everything works together for the good, life can then be enormously exciting for us.

I hope that at least some of what I have learned over my lifetime will be helpful to you.

Catherine A. Engel
Fort Collins, Colorado
April, 2017

PART ONE

The Journey

CHAPTER 1

How Did I Get Here?

Standing still.

When I was a kid, the very idea of standing still would have freaked me out. What? I can't run, and jump, and climb trees? I can't yell and scream when playing tag? Or singing? No singing? I have to be STILL? Are you crazy?

But from my (very) adult self, the idea doesn't seem crazy at all. Of course, we need to be still. Of course, we need silence. Of course, we have to turn the world off. Our very bodies are crying out for release from all the stimulation they get 24/7.

After all, our whole society is geared to so much noise, so much violence, in entertainment, YouTube, movies, and the constant 24-hour news loops, saying the same things over and over that just daily living becomes exhausting. If we're not texting, emailing, or posting our latest selfies on Facebook, there must be something wrong with us. We can't even put down our smart phones when we're driving, or having a quiet dinner with loved ones, or are at the movies. We have to let all our 749 friends know exactly what we had for breakfast, or that we are now in the produce aisle at the supermarket, as if they really care that we had oatmeal with strawberries again for the third day in a row.

I've been thinking about this idea of silence for a long time. I spent thirty years in the classroom, teaching elementary music to everyone from kindergarten to sixth grade, seventeen of those years in the same school. I got to know whole families of kids, siblings, and parents in the small town where I taught. I was even on the second generation of kids, whose parents I had taught when I first started out.

At first, that made me feel really old. But then I realized that that's what community feels like, when you know so many people, and how those Smith kids (names have been changed for privacy), all nine of them, are related to the Gomez family by marriage, and how in turn one of the Gomez kids married into the Robertson clan, who also had a whole string of youngsters I had taught. That feeling is like belonging to an extended clan, a tribe.

It felt good.

But one of the things about teaching music is that it is not a quiet profession. On the days when you have thirty beginning recorders playing out of tune, although you rejoice at their progress from day to day, it's really nice to get home, kick off your shoes, and just be.

There are always programs to prepare for, special field trips to sing or dance for nursing homes or at the Education offices, or Christmas performances at the local mall. Teaching music is like being on a merry-go-round. A new class appears every twenty-five minutes, and you as the teacher have to be as fresh and alive, with as much energy for that two-o'clock class as you were when you started at eight this morning. It can be exhausting.

By 1984, when I had been at it for nineteen years, I caught a cold that I just couldn't shake. I would force myself out of bed every morning, drag through my day, which sometimes also included staff meetings at seven a.m. and music teachers' meetings after school until five or five-thirty. But the cold lingered on, and I had used up all my sick days by October.

I told my principal I was going to have to take a medical leave of absence, because there was no way I could continue like this. He was very supportive, and helped me set it up with the district so that a substitute teacher could be hired until second semester.

Then began the round of doctors, none of whom had any idea what was wrong with me. They said it was mono, or maybe MS, or what about a brain tumor? They ran test after test, none of them conclusive. But I was tired and rundown, and I felt lousy all the time.

Finally our family doctor suggested I see a massage therapist to relieve my stress. I liked her a lot, and she turned out to be intuitive about a lot of things that were going on emotionally. She recommended going back to the doctor to see if maybe something like biofeedback might help.

It did. For a while.

Fortunately, the biofeedback doctor also was a psychotherapist, and I had a number of sessions with him, which helped somewhat, but all he could offer was talk therapy, and I didn't feel like that was exactly what I needed. So back to my family doctor I went. This time he gave me the name of a team of allergists, because, since nothing else had worked, maybe I had some kind of weird allergy.

The allergy clinic really turned out to be a Godsend because the doctors there were willing to keep looking until they found a treatment that worked.

One of the allergists had a colleague at National Jewish Hospital in Denver who was doing work with a new disease called the Yuppie Flu, or Epstein-Barr virus. This disease struck mostly young, successful professional people, and the treatment was IV gamma globulin infusions once a month. It was quite expensive, but I had good insurance through my school district, so I was willing to try it. At this point I would have tried almost anything, because I was desperate to find a cure.

The first time I got the infusion was the first time anyone had gotten this treatment in Fort Collins. Nobody was quite sure what to expect, so the staff had oxygen tanks at the ready, and the nurse was still reading the manual on how to do the procedure when I arrived.

Not exactly a confidence builder!

The miracle was that the IV gamma globulin treatment did work. However, the school district then switched to another insurance company that refused to pay for the treatments, and my husband and I couldn't manage the steep cost on our own. So I had to quit taking them.

For a while though, several years in fact, I did well without them.

When my health improved I got excited about the Orff Schulwerk method of teaching, a hands-on way of teaching that involved singing, games, dancing, story-telling, composition, playing many instruments, and a lot of ear-training. It was magic.

I finished four levels of the Orff training, and I became something of an expert in the field. I started giving workshops to teachers, which I enjoyed immensely, but it involved some traveling, and of course, teaching on weekends in addition to my regular course load.

And then, once again, the virus hit me, hard. Now they were calling it Chronic Fatigue Syndrome for the lack of energy, with fibromyalgia for the pains. There are eighteen pressure points on the body to test for fibromyalgia, and I had sensitivity and pain in all of them.

Clearly, this was way more than just a physical ailment; there was also an emotional component involved. That had not been recognized in 1984, which was at the beginning of the studies done by Dr. Herbert Benson, Joan Borysenko, Bernie Siegel, and others who were pioneers in the study of the mind-body connection. However, by 1996 the medical community was becoming aware that they did not have all the answers, and that some of the so-called "alternative" modalities, such as acupuncture, chiropractic, and massage could offer relief when doctors could not.

I quit my teaching job so that I could heal and tried them all, among them a treatment using energy work called The Alexander Method. There was no practitioner here in Fort Collins, so when a woman from Chicago who taught the method came for a three-week period to teach here, I jumped at the chance to learn from her.

In my first meeting with her she said, "You have holes in your aura." Now I didn't even know what an aura was, much less why I would have holes in it. But she began to teach me how to gather energy from around my physical body and bring it in close, especially around my left leg and upper body.

It turns out that we have several layers that make up what we think of as our "body". Not all of them are visible. The aura is the first level out from the physical body, and it extends about three feet in all directions, front, back, both sides, above, and below, much like an invisible bubble.

Later, after the Chicago teacher left, I learned that the Chinese system of Qi Gong moves energy in much the same way. I bought a DVD and taught myself at least the basics. Tai Chi works somewhat the same way, by moving energy around. This study led me to all kinds of interesting and exciting classes that I took locally about how to manipulate energy. Through these studies I met a lot of really interesting people whose world view was very different from mine.

The idea of healing with energy is ancient. The words *chi* and *qi*, both pronounced "chee," mean "life force" or "energy." So the idea of moving energy to heal someone from illness is one of the oldest methods of healing in the world. I had sort of intuited that energy work could help in healing, but I didn't really know what I was doing.

When my father lay dying in a Kansas City hospital in 1974 I had tried unsuccessfully to send healing energy to him when he was in a coma. I didn't understand then why it didn't work and he died anyway, in spite of my best efforts to help him get well. What I didn't know then was that it won't work unless the person wants to be healed. If they are already in the process of dying and accept it, then you must let them go. In order for healing to take place, the person must want to get well. Otherwise nothing you do in the way of sending them healing energy will help.

I think this is probably why when Jesus healed someone, He first always asked them what they wanted Him to do. He understood that He could only work a miracle if the person wanted Him to do it.

So I learned a lot during this time, but it still took a good two years of quiet time at home for me to heal. During this period, silence was my constant friend. I didn't go out much, because even the energy of a coffee shop or the ambient noise of the mall was too much stimulation.

What I needed was to stand still and let my body and mind heal.

CHAPTER 2

Growing Up

I grew up in a small Kansas town during World War II. My father, who had taught music at the local high school, had been drafted into the Navy, so my mother went back to work as a secretary, and we moved in with her parents, my grandparents.

My mother left for her job at the Abilene Flour Mill, Grandpa was an accountant who also did taxes in the spring, which left me at home with Grandma.

One of my favorite memories of that time, before I started school, was sitting on Grandma's lap at around five o'clock each evening, while we waited for the others to come home for dinner. My grandmother lived before it was fashionable to be slim and trim, and she loved to cook. So her body was softly rounded, all the better for me to snuggle up against while we waited for the rest of the family.

I don't remember talking during that time of waiting; it was just a time to be quiet and enjoy each other's company. So another benefit of standing, or in this case, sitting still, was to soak up the love that came in abundance from my wonderful grandmother.

Stillness allowed my childlike mind to wander wherever it wanted, watching the birds in the trees in our neighborhood, listening to the soft creaking of the rocking chair, smelling the powdery scent of my grandmother, hearing the sounds of older children in the neighborhood as they ran and played before coming inside for supper.

One of the problems teachers today face with their students is that kids don't have time to just wonder about the world. They are so used to being entertained every single minute of their day that they don't build the mental muscles they need to imagine things about the world. In my view, this is a huge problem.

I vividly remember, even as far back as the 1990s, asking my classes to come up with story ideas for which we could then write music and dances. The plan was that this performance would be completely designed and produced by the kids themselves. I had seen another teacher in a different school do this project with her kids, and it was great. However, the only suggestions I got from my students were rehashes of TV shows or movies they had seen, nothing original, even though I gave them several ideas to get them started. Their imaginations hadn't been developed, because they were always watching what someone else had created, not something they had dreamed up themselves. The fundamental problem, as I see it, is that no one—not adults, and certainly not kids—ever takes the time to just be still and wonder about the universe.

When I was a kid, there was no TV, there were no iPads or cell phones on which the children of today play games or watch movies nearly nonstop. We had time to dream. We could lie in the grass in the backyard and look at the clouds in the sky, imagining what shapes we could see above us.

In the summer, we could see a sky full of stars and wonder about where they all were, how far away. I have a memory of riding in the car at night after spending the day with Grandma's sister Lillie, who lived in Solomon, a small town west of Abilene. I must have been about ten, because Daddy was back from the Navy and was driving the car. I was sitting next to the window in the back seat, and as I looked out on the wondrous sky I felt so close to him, because I knew how much he loved the stars, too.

This memory is one I still summon up when I want to feel close to my dad, who has been dead for more than thirty years now.

There was time then, in the 1950s, to climb trees and marvel at the cherries growing there. There was time to lie on your stomach in the grass and watch the small bugs going about their buggy business.

About a block from my house was a vacant lot. The kids on my block, all twenty-three of the ones under the age of twelve or so, had to walk by this lot on the way to and from school every day. Usually on the way home, which was when we had more time, we would creep into this wondrous space, which we called The Jungle.

It was vacant, but it was far from empty. There were weeds as high as a second-grader's armpit, and we imagined all kinds of adventures there. The lot had several big trees, which made the space shady and mysterious, so we could pretend we were in a cave, or underwater in the sea, or on a pirate ship, or in an ancient forest where Robin Hood might be lurking with his band of Merry Men.

I don't remember talking there. Talking would have been sacrilegious somehow, and anyway, we didn't want to rile up any evil spirits who might be hanging around just waiting for unsuspecting kids to fall into their clutches. If there was any talking at all, it would have been in a furtive whisper. Who knew what might attack us if it knew we were there?

So again, silence played a big role in our stealthy games, which were nonetheless creative and extremely satisfying. They were the highlight of at least some of our schooldays that were otherwise occupied with the drudgery of math problems and learning state capitals.

To this day I love to walk, both in our neighborhood and hiking in nearby Rocky Mountain National Park, and for the most part, I prefer to be alone, so that I can use the time as a peaceful meditation on the beauty that surrounds me. Our neighborhood is hilly and filled with lovely homes and gardens. It is a constant joy to see the unfolding of the seasons in the blooming flowers and trees, listening to and watching birds, and smelling the freshness of the air.

You never know who or what might show up.

One day last summer my husband Pedro and I were hiking the Fern Lake Trail in Rocky Mountain National Park when suddenly there was a pack of mules carrying lumber to repair a bridge on the trail ahead of us that had been washed out in a recent flood. There were two guys on horseback, one at the head of the line and the other bringing up the rear, to make sure the mules got where they were going. What a lovely surprise for us! It wasn't a sight you see every day.

Our neighborhood is home to a huge flock of Canada geese. There are several ponds within a few blocks, and still some vacant land, so the geese love to feed on our grasses and plants. They know they are welcome and that no one will hurt them, so it's not unusual to see a flock of twenty or so in the middle of the street, crossing from one side to the other, e-v-e-r so slowly, one at a time. Cars wait patiently for the flock to waddle across, knowing it's futile to honk at them to go any faster. If perchance some impatient driver does dare to honk, the geese will half-heartedly rise a foot or so off the ground, then return unconcernedly to their meandering pace.

There is a Catholic church not too far from where I live which has an enormous lawn in front that slopes down to a major street. One Sunday I was leaving after Mass when I saw maybe five hundred geese milling around the front lawn, feeding. All at once, as if by a pre-arranged signal, they all took wing at the same time. The sound of their wings as they rose together into the sky was as I imagine the sound of angel wings might be. It was one of those breath-caught-in-the-throat-with-wonder moments, when all you can say is OHHHHH. It almost sounds like AWWWWWE.

How sad if we were never to experience awe.

And we can only have those peak moments if we are willing to be silent.

CHAPTER 3

Learning to Stand

We all know how hard it is for babies to learn to walk. First comes the scootching around on the baby's bottom or crawling, followed by grabbing hold of coffee tables, chair seats, or whatever else is handy that allows the child to hang on while learning to balance, and then finally—finally!—standing solo for a moment before plopping back down on the floor with a surprised look.

It is the same for us as we learn to stand in our own skin, with our own choices and our own desires springing forth as we grow into our own true being. There are times for learning throughout our lives, and many of them involve just standing still.

I can still remember learning to do the washing by watching Grandma every Monday morning. She was of the old school that said: " Monday is wash day, Tuesday is for ironing the clothes you washed the day before," and so forth during the week. Saturday, for instance, was for doing the baking, the grocery shopping, for catechism classes in the morning and confession in the afternoon.

Learning to do the washing wasn't as simple then as it is now. The washing machine was a cumbersome contraption with a wringer on the top of the tub. I was cautioned every week about not getting my fingers caught in the wringer. It would be very painful at best, and at worst I could lose a finger. Four-year-old fingers are so very small and fragile, after all.

So I stood nearby, next to Grandma, and watched carefully to see how she added the bluing to make the sheets and pillowcases white as snow. The bluing came in a little bottle, and you had to add a bit at a time to make sure you had the correct amount. Too much and the sheets would actually turn a bright blue; too little, and they wouldn't get that brilliant white that my grandmother was aiming for. You had to measure carefully. I was not allowed to do this job.

All I really could do was to stand by Grandma's side and learn. So that's what I did, but I still remember the joy of standing next to her and learning to be a big girl at her side.

Standing still as a learning posture is one we hardly ever think about, yet it is one of the most ancient methods of learning there is. From the days of Socrates, Plato and Aristotle standing, or sitting on the grass, was a time-honored way of gathering knowledge.

During the Middle Ages the apprentice stood close to the master to learn how to cut stone, paint pictures, and build houses. Then, under close supervision, the learner would gradually be able to do some of the tasks himself. Eventually, when the master thought the student was ready, he might be given the chance to show what he could do on his own before becoming a master himself and passing what he had learned to a new generation.

In my own life, I think of the days one summer when I tried and tried to learn how to dive into the water while standing on the side of the swimming pool. Over and over I would just belly flop ignominiously flat on my stomach without ever getting the hang of it. It certainly wasn't from lack of trying; I had many people attempting to help me, without success.

Finally, in desperation, my friend Joyce took matters into her own hands. She dived into the clear, sparkling, inviting water gracefully, but told me to wait on the side of the pool.

I stood there, half nervous, half excited, wondering what she would do.

She grabbed my ankles and held on tightly, making sure to tell me to keep my head down so that it would go into the water first. When I started my regular ungainly attempt, she held on and held on, and when she felt me going toward the water, she did a backwards somersault, letting the weight of my body carry her around, which caused me to avoid the dreaded belly flop.

I did it!

Oh, the joy, the satisfaction of FINALLY conquering something that had defeated me and my swimming teachers all summer long!

From then on, there was no stopping me. All throughout the rest of that summer I learned balance, and confidence, and I gained strength from the knowledge that I could do something for myself.

It was a huge learning, and I only learned it by standing still and trusting that the person holding my feet would not let me down. Joyce didn't let go until she knew I could do it on my own.

Sometimes all you can do to help someone else is to help them to hold on until they are able to do the task, or to stand with them through a difficult period in their life.

What a great gift to give someone else!

I belong to a rather small parish with many middle-aged and elderly people. It's not unusual to have someone in crisis because illness or death has touched their family.

About a year ago, one of our members, a lovely woman we had all known for years, was diagnosed with colon cancer. It had already advanced to the stage where she and her husband felt that they needed to move to Denver in order to be closer to their children, as well as to the doctors who would be caring for the stricken woman.

The Sunday before she and her husband left for their new home, the members of our parish gathered to pray for her healing and to ask for blessings on her and her family. The priest asked her to stand in the middle of the circle, with all of us standing around her with our hands touching her or at least touching someone who was closer to her than we were.

In this way, we all formed a circle of oneness and solidarity in standing with the sick person, letting her feel in a very tangible way how much we all cared about her. Many of us were in tears at the outpouring of love that we felt. It was a supremely emotional and graced moment to be able to share this healing ceremony with one another.

Later that same summer I was privileged to receive that same outpouring of love from the community when my husband was also diagnosed with colon cancer. He needed to have chemo and radiation, as well as two surgeries. Every week someone would offer prayers for his healing, or ask me how he was doing. It was a time for me to feel uplifted by so many people. Thank God for their support during what was a very difficult time in our life, as the community united in standing with us in prayer.

I think this way of learning is a gift that God gives to us, over and over throughout our lives. We so often have challenges that we don't know how to deal with, or problems we think we can't solve. But if we just stand still and let go of thinking that we can solve the difficulty all by ourselves, then God has a space to work inside us and to help us find the answers we have been looking for. The situation doesn't need to be as dramatic as cancer; it only needs to be something we can't seem to solve on our own.

When I was a young teacher, my school district had a mentoring program for newbies. A first-year teacher was paired with a veteran who was to be available to help solve problems that came up in the classroom. It was a wonderful program, because no matter how excellent your student teaching experience had been, it simply couldn't prepare you for the myriads of things that come up as a matter of course during that first school year when you are the person in charge.

That's when the mentor could step in and say, "I had a similar problem in my school, and this is how I handled it. Do you think it might work in your situation?"

Here again, it's a matter of standing next to people who really know what they are doing, and learning from them. My school district encouraged teachers to learn from one another and would give us professional days to visit someone else's classroom to see how they did things.

One of the things I learned from watching another teacher, for example, was how to deal with taking attendance for choir, which was scheduled during the lunch hour. Since she had limited time for rehearsal, she didn't want to spend a lot of precious minutes calling roll, so she came up with a sign-in sheet that was left on a chair in the hall. The only thing students had to do was to put a check mark next to their name each time they rehearsed. No muss, no fuss, and that took care of taking roll.

It seems like a very simple solution, and it was. I just would not have thought of it on my own.

Another master teacher taught me how to break lesson plans down into easy-to-learn segments, so that I could assess right away whether or not the students are getting what I thought they're getting. Just because I knew what I was teaching didn't always translate into the kids' getting the point of the lesson.

Once I thought I was really nailing my lesson plan with a group of first graders. A sweet little boy started waving his hand wildly, and I thought, thought I, innocently, "Oh, wow! I've really done it this time!"

And then he said, his face shining with happiness, "Guess what? My cat had kittens last night!"

So there you are. So much for masterful teaching!

I often encouraged group compositions, whether musically, or in writing a poem, or in figuring out a dance or an instrumental accompaniment. Groups of four or five students would stand or sit in a circle and come up with creative ideas, and for the most part, this method worked quite well.

Standing in the circle made a lot of sense if the group was working on a rhythmic pattern that needed stamping, clapping, swaying, or turning. Sitting together might work better if they were brainstorming ideas for the words to a song they were writing. The kids could always figure out which method worked better for them.

Standing next to someone else in the circle came to mean standing *with* others, and that's a valuable lesson for all of us to learn, for in the end, we all learn from one another. Life is not a spectator sport, and it's also a lot more fun if we can learn to do it together.

I vividly remember being at a music educators' conference when the presenter was the late great brain researcher, Don Campbell. He had spent the hour talking about the Mozart effect, which at the time was a popular idea about how to increase academic learning by playing Mozart to young children. The thing that was new was that some of the overtones in the music were removed, which allowed the sounds to access different parts of the brain than would otherwise have been utilized.

It had been a stimulating and thought-provoking session, and Don brought it to a close by having us move into a long double line holding hands with the people on either side of us. The two lines were then joined by a person at the end of each line who connected the lines into a long, very narrow circle. The shape ended up being sort of like a long sausage.

We were to look deeply into the eyes of the person across from us, and then take one side-step to the left. As we got to the end of our line, the person on the end would not have a partner until he or she moved around the end place in the circle to the other line. This meant that we would never look directly into the eyes of the person on either side of us, but they were the only ones with whom we had direct physical contact. So in fact, we all really were connected, either by physical touch or by looking into another person's eyes.

For most of the people in the group, my experience was to smile and greet them silently and move on. But there was one woman, whom I had never seen before and never saw again, with whom the soul connection was so deep I felt as if I had known her forever. It was one of those inexplicable moments that has stayed with me for twenty years or more.

Standing still can be an incredible blessing. It can help us learn to stand on our own two feet, or to support someone else who is having a difficult time. It can help us remember that we're not alone, but that we have others to help us and to stand with us in times of trial.

What a gift that turns out to be.

CHAPTER 4

Standing Up

Baby steps are a good beginning, but that's all they are, a first step. If we never learned how to move forward, we would never make any progress, either in learning to walk, or more importantly, in our lives. So how do we learn to move from the toddler stage into a more grown-up posture?

Of course, a lot of what we learn comes naturally, just through our day to day experience, and we don't give those new experiences much thought. They just happen. All at once, we are two years old, cruising all over our own house, then before we know it, we're five and starting kindergarten.

For most of my generation, kindergarten was our first experience dealing with people other than our own family or the kids who lived in our neighborhood. Hardly any of the moms worked, except for my own mother. My situation was unique, and was possible only because we lived with my grandparents, which allowed my mom to be out in the workplace while my grandmother stayed at home with me. No one went to daycare or babysitters—that word hadn't even been invented in the 1940s. Thus for a small child, meeting twenty-five or thirty other kids in an institutional setting was often upsetting and very scary.

I remember worrying about my first day at school for several weeks ahead of time, until Mom assured me that it would be a new adventure, and it was only for kids who were big enough. It was not for babies.

So, even though I knew I would have to give up sucking on my fingers when I was nervous so as not to look like I was not old enough to be in school, I was also excited to get to go to a place where I would meet new kids and make friends. Mom promised me that all this newness would be fun. I believed her. However, school is not always fun for kids who are shy and retiring.

I vividly remember that when I was teaching there was a little girl in kindergarten who was so traumatized that she never spoke a word. I was very worried about her; so was her teacher, who called and arranged for the parents to come in for a conference. Lo and behold, the parents didn't speak much either. They were not new immigrants or anything like that, they simply didn't say anything.

So this poor little girl had never had good speech habits modeled for her, and she was totally overwhelmed by all the stimulation. This was a new, scary place that had lots of kids who loved to talk, who wanted to talk all of the time, and who couldn't understand why she didn't join in their games or banter. I felt so sorry for her. It took her until Thanksgiving before she felt confident enough to stand up for herself and utter a few words in front of the class. Being a somewhat shy person myself, I totally understood how she must have felt.

In fact, I have a distinct memory of my own that is very similar to what this little girl was probably going through. In this memory, I am about six or so, very tall for my age. I see myself standing at the very back of a group of first graders, feeling awkward and shy, unsure of myself. The rest of the kids are talking to the teacher about something that must have happened on the playground at recess. I'm not sure why this is such a scary memory, only that I think

I hadn't seen exactly what had happened, and so I didn't want to get involved for fear of making a mistake.

I have no memory of the actual conversation, only about the intense fear and how cold my hands were. I did not join in with the others in speaking. In fact, all I wanted to do was to stand perfectly still and hope that no one would notice I was there. I was terrified.

Speaking up in this case would have been the most frightening thing I could imagine. Luckily, I don't remember anything else about that scene, even whether or not I had to speak up. Probably I didn't, because surely I would remember if I had had to step out of my comfort zone to make a comment.

But gradually, through many months of being in first grade, and realizing that I was at least as smart if not smarter than a lot of my classmates, I began to find my voice. I started raising my hand to read out loud, because I was a good reader, and I knew that it was a job I could handle. When I knew the answer to a question the teacher asked, I raised my hand. I was beginning to show up in my own life.

Then I got sick with the German measles. Nowadays, when most children are vaccinated against this dreadful disease, it is rare for whole classes of kids to be exposed to this kind of illness. But in the 1950s there were no vaccines. So parents and kids alike suffered through the "childhood diseases" since we had no other choice. Consequently, many kids in my class got sick.

The treatment was that I had to be still in a darkened room so as not to lose my eyesight. It lasted for an agonizing three weeks, and I itched like crazy. Of course, all the adults said, "You mustn't scratch; it will cause scars on your body." But OF COURSE I wanted to scratch! I *itched*, for heaven's sake! It was torture.

When the doctor finally cleared me to go back to school, I was once again terrified. Even though the class had made cards for me with their good wishes for my speedy recovery, I was afraid of what they might say when I went back to class. The old shyness returned, and I didn't want to go back at all.

The fear of returning was almost as much of a torture as the disease had been. The feeling was the same as it had been when I had been afraid to go to school for the first time. But in the end my mother insisted that these children were my friends and that they would welcome me back with open arms. She was right.

By second grade, I had discovered that I could sing, and that it was fun. My second-grade teacher, Miss Thompson, was a kind, grandmotherly sort of person, and she loved me almost as much as my real grandmother did. I would have done anything to please her.

So when it was time for the Christmas program, all the second-grade classes in town were to perform together at the City Auditorium downtown. We took school buses to the rehearsals, and once again, I was going to be the center of attention. This time I was both scared and elated to have been chosen to be the star on the very tiptop of the living Christmas tree.

I was (am still) scared of heights, and here I was, having to climb up many rickety rows up to the top of the wooden tree frame. It was probably a good ten to twelve feet above the stage, and I was going to be the only one up there, wearing a golden crown with a star on top as a headpiece. My heart pounded every time I had to make that scary climb, but I did it. There's something to be said for doing the thing that frightens us until the repetition itself helps us to grow accustomed to the feeling. It eventually loses its power to terrorize us and becomes familiar, if not exactly natural.

At the same time, my beloved teacher, Miss Thompson had discovered that I could sing harmony, and she encouraged me to sing harmony on some of the carols. Somehow it was far less terrifying to sing harmony than it was to speak up for myself or climb that rickety tree, because I knew I could sing well.

Singing was a way for me to let my voice be heard. I knew no one was going to make fun of me for being too tall, too awkward, too gangly when I sang. I had a clear, true voice, and music was something I loved.

My family was very musical, and there was music in our house for as long as I can remember. My father, who had a beautiful bass voice, had taught vocal music at the local high school before the War, and my mother played piano by ear for two service organizations, the Lions and the Rotary Clubs. My grandfather was also a pretty good country fiddler who had grown up in Kentucky, the home of bluegrass, both the plant and the music. He never had a lesson in his life, but he had a good ear, and he could pick up a song very quickly if he heard it once.

By sixth grade I was learning to play both the piano and the cello, so we had many impromptu musical evenings in those days before television. It was fun, and it fostered a closeness within our family that children today may never experience.

It's one thing to be in your own room, plugged in to your own computer, or iPhone, or tablet, or watching your own favorite TV show by yourself, away from the rest of your family. It is quite another to be engaged in a common activity such as singing around the piano, or playing your own version of chamber music with those you love and live with. Somehow I think that families that interact with each other are stronger and more resilient, both in good times and the ones that aren't so good, than families who rarely see one another.

When we share mealtimes together, we naturally find time to share stories about what's going on in our lives right now, how we feel about current events, and the people we know at school and at work. We learn that our lives are important. We learn to rely on one another, and that the people we love the most have our backs in the difficult times.

And in the end, don't we all long for that kind of connection? Don't we all want to be part of a community of people who share our interests and who want the best for us? That's how we learn to stand on our own two feet. We need the support of those we love to help us discover how to stand up by ourselves. When we have that kind of support behind us, we find that we can weather almost anything.

CHAPTER 5

Standing in Trust

When I was little, I went to catechism classes every Saturday morning at St. Andrew's Catholic Church in Abilene. The Baltimore Catechism was our study guide, which we had to memorize completely, as it covered all the beliefs and practices one needed to live a good Catholic life.

I remember that the very first question was "Who made me?" The answer, fittingly enough was, "God made me," which to my six- or seven-year old mind made perfect sense.

The second question was similar: "Why did God make me?" "To know, love, and serve Him in this life and to be happy forever with Him in the next."

Well, duh. Who didn't know that? I just took it for granted that everyone else in the whole world thought exactly as I did.

But that was then. The answers that came so easily when I was a child have been tempered by real life experience, and now I know that nothing is as simple as it seemed to me to be as it was at that age. Then, in that simpler time, I was sure I had all the answers. God seemed to me to be a given in life, and I knew exactly who He was, and what He wanted from me.

Now I am often not so sure. When I was a kid, life was pretty much a black-and-white deal, with little or no room for improvisation or choices. With personal knowledge I now understand that often life is lived more in the gray areas, which are infinitely bigger in scope, but things are also far less sure to me than they seemed then. So much of what we are looking for seems to depend on how much we trust: ourselves, others, and especially God.

Why is it that the longer I live, the less sure I am about anything? Possibly it is because many of us sometimes fail to do the things we set out to do, or we are disappointed with the way things turn out, even if we thought we knew what we were doing at the time. Our lives became complicated, almost without our noticing.

So long as we were operating from a more or less tribalistic point of view, we knew who we were and what we should do with our lives. However, if as we grew in knowledge and experience we came across other people whose ideas and values were different from that of our kith and kin, we began to see that things were not the same for everyone around the world. The advent of jet travel, which allows people to see new places and experience new ideas, has taught us that the old ways are not the only ways at all.

Before World War II, women were not used to being the ones in charge. For most girls a college education may have been beyond their reach, because many families subscribed to the idea that women didn't need to be educated. What was the use of paying for higher education if the girl was just going to get married and have babies? The husband would always take care of the family, after all. But for far too many women, that was not the way it was. With no man to depend on, women learned that they were the ones who had to work, and they found out that they were good at it.

So things changed, and the world and the old ideas changed, too.

Nowadays, girls—and boys, too—have many options as to their choice of field of study and whether to marry young, wait until they are older, or not get married at all. Their options seem endless.

But that doesn't mean that our emotional makeup has grown up alongside all of these changes. Just because we have more opportunities than our parents did does not make us any the more secure or sure of what we should be doing with the rest of our lives.

It takes a lot of trust just to live.

It must have been much that way for Mary and Joseph when Jesus was born. Here they were, a young Jewish couple following the pattern that most families of their time did. They got engaged and were planning to get married, but before that could happen, Mary found herself to be pregnant.

Now in those days being unmarried and pregnant was a serious offense, one that could get the girl stoned to death for adultery. Pretty serious stuff for a fourteen-year-old to have to deal with. We can only imagine her fear and worry. No matter that she said an angel had appeared to her and told her what was going to happen. She was terrified. What should they do next? How could they go about making this horrible situation right? How could she trust that God really would have her back?

But Joseph relied on God, and then a strange thing happened. He had a dream in which an angel appeared to him and told him not to worry. Mary had not done anything wrong, but by the power of the Most High she had been chosen to bear a son who would lead his people Israel. Joseph was assured that he should go ahead and marry Mary, but to do it quietly and without a lot of fuss.

So that is what they did. They trusted that God knew what was going on, even if they didn't have a clue.

Sometimes when we are faced with an impossible situation that is all that we *can* do. We have to trust God to help us, because we are at a total loss as to know how to deal with the situation. Our puny attempts to make things work may just leave us so flummoxed that we don't even know where we are, or how to begin to solve the problem. I recently had a situation—not one as dire as Mary and Joseph faced, to be sure—but one that I didn't know how to fix. I stewed about it and wondered and tried various things, none of which worked in the least, but it was only when our parish priest gave a stirring homily the first week of Advent about how Mary and Joseph had not had a users' manual to figure out what they should do about their critical and possibly life-ending situation that the whole thing clicked for me.

I don't have a users' manual either, and maybe the answer to my problem was the same as it was for them. I needed to trust that God would show me what was to come next. And I had to trust my own instincts as a spiritual seeker.

Trust. Such a simple word, and yet so hard to put into practice! It has become almost a cliché that when I hear the words, "Trust me," I invariably do just the opposite. Why should I trust someone who may not know any better than I do what is right for me? "You're not the boss of me!" I want to shout. "I am my own best expert!"

While all that may be true, just then I needed some help, and I was too close to the situation to see what the solution should be.

Enter Father Jim and his marvelous homily. Aha, thought I, now I know what this situation needs. It has to be about trust. Trust in God, and trust in myself, that I do have the answers inside myself if I just slow down enough to hear what God is telling me.

And that is where the standing still part comes in again. We have to take the time and make the space for God to work within us. Even during the Advent/Christmas spending frenzy, when we are bombarded with all the TV ads about all the things we need and all the sales on Black Friday, Small Business Saturday, and Cyber Monday, we need to stop and listen.

Trust in God is not easy for most of us. Trust in general is not easy for many of us. We like to think that we are the boss, and that we know best. And much of the time that is absolutely true. But there is a difference between our ego wanting to run the show and our small, interior voice that is the voice of our soul.

How can we tell the difference?

If our ego is the one in control, we may feel a sense of pride, something that puffs us up and makes us want to brag about how great we are. That's not the kind of trusting that I am talking about here. The trust I mean is in understanding that God works through us, using our own intellect and instincts to know what is right for us to do.

For example, sometimes we get an inner sense about whether something is right or wrong for us. I once dated a guy in college who was cute, tall, and a good dancer. We had a lot of fun together, and I liked his sense of humor. But he had a dark side, too, one that included using uppers and downers, which he freely told me about. But I was naïve, and I just sort of let the rather "off" feeling I had about him slide without doing anything about it. He had told me in a sort of joking way, and I wasn't even sure about what "bennies" were. Not then. Drug use was not so common then, at least not with any of the people I knew, and the whole idea just sort of went over my head.

We were good friends with another couple, people I had known a long time, and we often double-dated with them. I thought that if something was really wrong, they would surely have picked up on it, but no one said a word about it. In any case, three of the four of us had no experience with any kind of drug use, since it was just not common in central Kansas in the 1960s. I doubt that any of us would have known what to do about it even if we had suspected that my boyfriend was using.

Anyway, after I had dated this guy for nearly a whole school year, he was arrested for stealing property from the company he worked for. I thought at first that it must be a mistake. How could he be in jail? I had met his parents and knew that his dad was a Methodist minister. Weren't they all good people? But the fact was, he was in jail pending a trial, and he might be facing doing real time in prison.

This whole situation was so far from my natural habitat, so to speak, that I was totally out of my depth. I had no one I could turn to. My mother would have been aghast had I had the temerity to tell her, which of course I didn't.

So I stewed over the situation for a while all by myself. Our good friend Daniel was about as straight a shooter as I could hope to find, and he turned out to be a great source of comfort. He took over ferrying me back and forth to a town where I had had a role in a summer theater play until we both tired of the strain it put on our friendship.

I had thought I would be devastated at this unceremonious breakup with a man with whom I was already talking marriage, but that didn't happen. I felt nothing but relief, relief that I had dodged a bullet and a situation that was bound to be bad at some time down the line. I just had been so besotted that I wasn't able to see it clearly before.

Once I had turned my former romance over to God and let go of any particular outcome, the whole scenario resolved itself easily and happily, at least for me. I never did find out what happened with the guy in jail. Nor did I care. He had broken the trust I had had in him.

However, trust in God is not always simple. When we ask God for something we are not always sure that He will give us what we request. He has a much broader perspective than we do, and He can see when giving us what we ask for would bring us harm or otherwise not be good for us in the long run. While He respects and honors our freedom to ask Him for whatever we want, He does not always grant us the favor we ask for.

Sometimes the gift we are given is much bigger and better than the small thing we had proposed to Him. He is a generous God, after all, and He knows what we are really asking for, even if what we seem to want might not be the big and wondrous thing He has in mind for us.

I am thinking back to one of the most significant occurrences in my life. It happened after a major upset in the church that I had attended for over thirty years. Our whole congregation was in an uproar about the new priest who was dictatorial, unbending, and totally unable or willing to listen to parishioners' complaints. A large number of people finally left the parish, some even leaving the Roman Catholic Church over the hurt they felt. Even the assistant pastor finally asked for and received a transfer.

I also left that parish and went to another one which felt friendlier, but I still had many longstanding friends at the old church. While I was dithering around as to where I should go for Christmas Eve Mass we got seven inches of snow overnight two days before Christmas. I wasn't really paying attention the way I normally would have, and I came into our house with ice on my shoes, slipping and falling, breaking my knee and my arm in two places.

These injuries were so severe that I spent five days in the hospital before transferring to a rehab facility where I stayed until mid-February. In fact, my rehab lasted about six months, because even when I returned home I was in a wheelchair, with physical and occupational therapists who came to our house until the end of April. By the end of June I could once again drive a car and walk unassisted.

Now you could say that my fall was just an accident. But I knew why it really had happened; it was to get me away from the church situation so that I could get some clarity about what I was to do next. Here I was, looking for enlightenment and spiritual growth, and *that* was what I was really asking for, not just what Mass or what church to go to on Christmas Eve.

Of course, at the time I didn't see it that way at all. It took many months of reflection and meditation before I finally got to the "aha moment." But once I did finally understand the exquisite timing and orchestrating of the exterior event, it seemed like, well, of *course* it turned out the way it did. How could it have been otherwise? Had I just been able to trust God's goodness at the time, I would have saved myself a lot of grief. But maybe I wasn't supposed to get it all at once. Maybe it was intended all along to be *a process* that I had to go through in order to find the underlying message.

Most of us are not very good at trusting, either ourselves or God. It feels like we have to give up control, and most of us are programmed to be independent. Therefore, the idea of giving up control, even to God, is really, *really* scary, and it takes a lot of courage to hand over the reins to someone else.

We must step out of our normal comfort zone into the unknown, and most of us would rather deal with something we know, even if it doesn't make us happy, than to trust that the new thing will serve us better.

Families who escape from poverty and the violence of war to move to a new country are so courageous. Talk about having trust! How frightening it must be to leave everything they have ever known, without any certainty that the new place will welcome them. They must deal with learning a new language and customs while at the same time finding jobs and making a whole new life for themselves and their loved ones.

Mary and Joseph had to go through something similar when the angel told them to go to Egypt to escape Herod's slaughter of the children of Israel. The king was hoping to kill the baby Jesus, whom the Magi had said would be the new King of Israel. Herod was taking no chances that some youngster might one day replace him, so he ordered that all the boy babies under the age of two were to be put to death. Mary and Joseph were told by an angel in a dream that they were in danger and must leave Israel immediately.

Even if you are the Holy Family it still takes courage to leave the old place and the old ways, sometimes even leaving the rest of your family behind. It takes a lot of trust to forge your own path, but they trusted that God knew what was best for their safety, so they set off in the middle of the night to make their way by donkey to Egypt. They left in fear, but they trusted in God's wisdom to save them. This Gospel story appears in Matt: 2, 13-16.

Sometimes the leaving occurs when we must separate from the things that our families hold dear. These may be values or ideas that have been passed down from generation to generation, and it takes no less bravery to set out and go our own way than it does to leave the country of our birth. For most of us, before we can trust someone else we need to be clear about what it is we want for ourselves. One way to do that is to pray about it.

I don't ever remember specifically learning how to pray. It was just one of those things I took for granted. The children all just figured it out more or less by osmosis and by doing it over and over, imitating the adults as we went along until it was second nature to us. It was the same process a child uses when first starting to learn a language. We trusted that our parents and our teachers had our best interests at heart, so we did as we saw them doing.

We went to Mass every Sunday and holy day, and we learned the responses in Latin by hearing them over and over. We learned to pray the Rosary the same way, by hearing the prayers again and again until we too could use the correct words.

In the 1950s saying the Rosary was a big deal. Bishop Fulton J. Sheen had a weekly radio program whose catchphrase was, "The family that prays together stays together." He was one of the primary advocates of saying the Rosary as a family each night before bedtime, and while my family didn't pray together, there were plenty of other opportunities to meditate on the mysteries that represented the events in the life of Jesus.

Another factor in praying the Rosary was the Cold War. Pope Pius XII had recently released one of the so-called "secrets of Fatima" that Mary supposedly had given to three Portuguese shepherd children, and this secret was that Mary wanted us to pray the Rosary daily for the conversion of Russia.

So our Kansas parish organized the members by neighborhood, and every Wednesday night we went to one house or another to pray. I can still remember how grown up I felt when Agnes Wylder, one of my "holy old ladies" as I thought of the elderly women I looked up to, allowed me to lead the prayers. I must have been eight or nine years old, and I felt so honored to be chosen to be the leader, for that meant that Agnes must have had enough confidence in my knowledge of the process that she could trust me not to mess it up. I was in heaven!

On the nights when we didn't go to someone else's house, I dutifully took my rosary to bed with me and said at least one set of five mysteries before going to sleep. Often I fell asleep in the middle, but that was okay because my intention had been to spend time with God, and I did that even when I was asleep.

Prayer thus became a daily habit with me, and I still carry a rosary in my purse and keep another on my bedside table. That way I will always be prepared in case I feel the urge, although I must admit that I don't say the Rosary as much as I did when I was a child. My usual form of prayer is meditation nowadays, and I will say more about that in a later chapter.

In my third or fourth grade religion class, Sister Redempta had taught us to say a morning prayer offering our day to God when we first get up. To this day I continue to do it as part of my morning meditation, usually right at the very beginning.

There was a formal prayer that I have long since forgotten, because the words were somewhat stilted, with a lot of "vouchsafes" and "deign to grant us" sorts of words, words that I would never in a million years think of saying in real life. I mean, come on. Who uses language like that? I sure didn't.

So I make up my own prayer, something along the lines of, "Dear God, please bless my day today. Thank You for the good night's sleep and for this beautiful morning. Bless everything I do, and all the people I meet, especially those who are in special need of Your help today. Bless our world, and keep everyone safe and healthy. Thank You for Your loving care. Amen."

I keep our friends and neighbors in prayer, especially when they have challenges such as ill health or needing to find a job. Praying for others has been known to work miracles, and our world needs prayers now to deal with all the uncertainty and division we hear about every day on the news.

Prayer can be done at any time, alone or with others. We don't need to be in church, or kneeling down, or in any other special posture to pray. God hears us just the same.

Once when I was about five or six, I was sick in bed for several days. Grandpa, who was not a believer, came into my room one evening and asked me what I was doing. "Praying," I said, much to his surprise.

"Oh," he replied, "I thought you had to kneel down to do that."

Grandpa must have had enough of a religious background to have formed at least some rudimentary ideas about what prayer was, but clearly the idea of just talking to God informally wasn't one of them.

I find that I am often closest to God in the middle of the night when I can't sleep. That's when I turn my worries over to Him, just trusting that He will take care of everything while I'm at rest. Then usually I can fall asleep quickly and easily, but that only happens when I am willing to trust Him to take care of the details. I know that some people rarely pray, but I am not one of them. Prayer is what gets me through the day. If I make the intention that my whole life is to be a prayer, then I feel close to God at any time. I don't have to make a formal declaration for it to be true.

Prayer doesn't need to be of any particular religion; in fact, sometimes religion just obscures our relationship with the Divine. The very word "religion" comes from the Latin root that means "to re-connect or re-tie together," but sometimes it seems as if formal religion with all its rules and regulations about how to pray or to think about God just gets in the way of any true communion with Him. I often eschew formal religious prayers, because they don't end up saying what I want to say to the One Who Is the All. They say what somebody who is trying to be religiously correct thinks God wants us to say.

I just pray as I talk. I use incomplete sentences, stop and start, just as I would in real life if I'm having a conversation with a friend. I'm sure that He who is the Source of all understands what I am trying to say.

The whole thing boils down to whether or not I trust the Creator enough to have a relationship with Her. If I trust someone enough to have a relationship with him or her, then I know that it will take work to keep the friendship going. I can't just show up once every ten years or so and expect that it will be enough.

If we love somebody, we want to make time to be with them and to talk often. We share our lives. We trust that the other person will want what is best for us, even if we only meet in person every few years.

I have a good friend whom I only see once in every five years or so, but we keep in touch through Facebook and phone calls in between times. We've been friends since we were five, and we are now in our seventies. Both of us have had serious illnesses, she has outlived two husbands, and still we feel like we did when we first met in kindergarten.

Trust begins with us, but we must also know that the other person is trustworthy. Without trust there can be no love, and love is what it's all about. Just when we think we have life all figured out, we discover that we don't. Sometimes when we have trusted an occurrence or a person to be the thing we thought we most wanted, we find out that instead of gold, we have placed our faith in what is really just yellow paint.

It's especially hard when we want to place our trust in God, but instead our early experiences with church or synagogue or other faith teaching have hurt us badly. When we are angry and feeling used by religion, that's when trust becomes the most difficult for us.

So what are we to do when we feel the need to be trusting and yet trust is the one thing we can't seem to do?

The only thing I know for sure about trust is that our bodies will tell us if we are on the right track or not. How does a decision feel in our gut? Does it feel expansive or contractive, happy or nerve-wracking? If we always go for the good feeling, that is one way of knowing that we are in alignment with God. If it is loving and kind, it is right.

And isn't that what we all want deep down? Don't we want to both give and receive love? Don't we want to be treated with kindness and respect? I know that's what I want, and I suspect that most people would agree.

There is yet another type of trusting God that sometimes comes into play. We have some particular favor in mind, and we pray and pray for it, but nothing happens. "Aha," we say with disgust, "see? God doesn't always listen to our prayers at all. I think He's a fraud."

So what is really going on here? One possible answer is that we and God are on different wavelengths. We think we are asking for help in losing twenty pounds, but in the back of our minds there is a competing thought: "But does that mean I will have to give up ice cream? Hmm. Maybe I don't really want to lose that weight, after all. But surely God knows what I'm thinking, right? So I'll keep on asking Him to help me lose twenty pounds."

Now there is a kind of logic here at work that seems on the surface to be right in line with what we are asking for. We want to lose twenty pounds, but we are hooked on cookies and ice cream. Guess which thought is really going to be stronger? Yep, the one about having to give up the ice cream. Why? Because we are investing more energy into the thought about *not* getting ice cream than we are into the thought about losing the twenty pounds. There is a stronger emotional "kick" at the thought of doing without our favorite dessert than there is a good feeling about being twenty pounds lighter.

First, we have to get ourselves into a good-feeling place. It doesn't much matter what exactly we are thinking about, only that it makes us feel good. In fact, the better we feel, the more likely we are to get what we want, whether or not we pray for it. The more we can imagine the new way of being, the better our chances of actually getting what we want. We take time to see it in detail, with all the glorious colors and sounds, maybe feeling the soft breeze on our face, smelling the beautiful flowers, and picturing ourselves getting positive comments from others about how nice it will be once we have our heart's desire.

So let's say that the reason we want to lose the weight is so that we will have more energy and feel physically better. Perhaps weight loss will help us to play more energetically with our kids or our dog, and we will get to go to the park more often as a result. At the park we often run into other people who are also playing with their kids or their dogs, and we would love to become part of such a group. In addition, if we lose weight, we will be able to wear more stylish clothing and participate in many activities that once seemed to be too hard to do.

The more reasons we can find to be excited about our weight loss, the more likely we will be to actually make it happen. Being excited is the key element here. In order for the desire to come true, we must feel really positive and happy that we are now moving toward what it is that we want. In this scenario, it is easier to trust that we will achieve our goals, because now we are energetically lined up with what we want.

If our emotions do not resonate with what we are asking for, we'll never get it. Just as the snares on a drum resonate in sync with other instruments in the room, even if no one is playing the drum itself, the snares pick up the vibrations from those instruments and react accordingly. So too, we must resonate vibrationally with what we are trying to receive if we are to have any hope of achieving it. Otherwise, we will think that God does not hear our prayers, when it is actually that our inner being is not in sync with what we want.

Trust is easier when we know what we really want, but sometimes we don't know what that is.

So how do we learn to trust ourselves? The best way is to ask our inner self. Here is an easy test. When I first learned this technique, I tried doing it with something simple, such as which restaurant to choose. I would put one choice in my right hand and one in my left. Then I would ask myself how it felt if I chose the option in my left hand. Tuning in to how my body responded, I noticed if there was any tension in my gut. Did my hands sweat or my breathing feel strained? Did my shoulders tense up? Then I tried the other option. It usually was very clear in a matter of moments which one I preferred. If I didn't get a clear answer, then it probably didn't really matter one way or the other.

I have used this technique for all sorts of things when I am not sure about what I should do. It even works for the big things, like "Is it time to retire? Or should I stay another year at this school?"

Trusting oneself is one of the most important skills we will ever master, and once we can do it, our lives will be simpler and much more pleasant. We all have this innate wisdom inside ourselves; we just have to learn how to access it. It leads us to such freedom and joy when we know we are able to make the right decisions for our own lives.

Now instead of worrying about which decision to make, if we just ask ourselves what it is we really want, we find that choosing what we want and being clear about it is fun and easy. I think trusting God comes down to the same thing.

Here is where the stillness comes in again. If we take the time to quiet ourselves and tune in to our body and to the part of ourselves known as the soul or our Higher Self, often a question will resolve itself quickly and easily. But we have to put aside our worries of the day. Just get quiet. Stand still for a moment. Let trust enter into your very being.

In the Old Testament, God made a contract with the Jewish people by telling them, "You will be my people, and I will be your God." (Ex. 6:7.) That was an invitation to them to trust Him with their lives, much as lovers trust one another when they pledge to spend their lives together in marriage. It is a sacred contract, with both parties participating in the agreement. If there is true love involved, there will be trust on both sides.

When I think of all the good things God has given me in my life, even if things are not going the way I would ideally want them to, I can usually manage to find a way to trust Him to know what is best for me. God's perspective, after all, is so much larger than mine is that I'm sure He sees the big picture, whereas I am seeing only my small part in the grand scheme of things.

Trust is not easy, that's for sure, but when we have great love, it becomes a joy. The great 13th-century spiritual writer and mystic, Julian of Norwich, had a saying in the book *Showings* that she wrote about the visions that she had from God. I like it very much: "All will be well, and all will be well, and all manner of thing shall be well." Julian doesn't say that all will be well right now, only that things *will be* well in the end. In God's own time—sometime—all will be well. I trust that it will be so.

CHAPTER 6

Holding the Space

Sometimes being still does not involve doing anything at all. There are times that all we can do, either for ourselves or for someone else, is to hold the space so that the other person or life itself can do the heavy lifting.

Once when I was in college, I was in a dance troupe with about twelve or fifteen other girls. At Christmastime, the director of this group thought it would be exciting to do a complete telling of the Christmas story through dance. This was a Catholic girls' school in the 1960's, so there was no thought that our show might possibly offend someone by being too religious. Our audience would be the student body, plus the nuns and lay professors of our college, and we were mostly all Catholic.

One of the episodes in which I had a part was the reading from the Book of Wisdom 18:14, in which it says in part: "For while gentle silence enveloped all things, and night in its swift course was now half-gone, Thy all-powerful Word leaped down from heaven, from the royal throne. . . ."

I was playing the role of God the Father, and I was to stand on the top platform, which was about eight feet off the ground. (Here we go again with the high platform, just like the time in second grade when I had to be atop that living Christmas tree. This was getting to be a theme.)

My friend Joyce was dancing the part of Jesus, "the Word who leaped down from heaven." So naturally, she had to leap from the eight-foot platform down to another one which was about four feet off the ground. The lower part wasn't all that big, and it scared me every time she had to make that leap. I was so afraid that she would miss the platform altogether, or land wrong and break her leg or something worse, that it was all I could do to just stand there with my arms outstretched looking Godly and watch her make that jump.

Miraculously, or so it seemed to me, she never missed.

However, my job was not to help her jump, nor to make sure that she made the leap successfully. My job was simply to stand there looking benevolent, like God, and to hold the space for her to do her thing. It was one of the hardest things I have ever had to do.

The "dancing" part of it was so simple. All I had to do was to stand and to watch over her. But emotionally it was very difficult, because I would not have been able to catch her if she fell, nor could I have prevented her from falling. I could do nothing but stand still and watch.

Recently my husband had a rather serious surgery, and again I felt that same familiar out-of-control feeling that I had had while watching Joyce make that jump.

When people you love are fighting a serious illness, there is nothing you can do while they are in surgery. They are no doubt comfortably asleep while the doctors and nurses take care of the details. All that family members can do is to sit in the waiting room wondering nervously how things are going.

At times like these, many people turn to prayer to help them to get through the endless hours of waiting for news. I was no different. I, too, prayed—a lot. But regardless of whether or not I was praying, the nurses at the hospital were able to call my cell phone and let me know how things were progressing. They called several times during the nearly five-and-a-half hours the surgery took. I am very grateful to them for their kindness.

The waiting room was full that morning. As the time passed, ever so slowly it seemed to me, I watched others as they fell asleep on sofas, using their handbags as pillows and covering themselves with their sweaters. The hands on my watch moved tortoise-like from seven to eight to nine, and on into the afternoon hours, as all of us sat patiently on guard, holding the space for our loved ones.

But even when the operation was over and my husband had been moved to a room on the sixth floor of the hospital, there were endless days of waiting for enough healing to occur so that he could be discharged and return home.

Times like these are not under our control; there is nothing we can do to help the healing process. All we can do is to be there for the sick one, assisting as best we can by sending them healing energy, all the while knowing that the final result is ultimately up to God and the patient's own will to survive.

Surrendering to the process is hard work. We want so much to be in control of the situation; we want everything to be okay and to get our lives back to normal, but often the result is nothing like the old familiar way of living we had known before.

In my husband's case, the surgery involved removing the cancerous part of the intestine and installing a stoma, which as anyone who has one knows, changes your life forever. Yes, the cancer is gone, thank God, but learning to deal with a stoma is extremely difficult. Life for my husband is now very different from the way it had been for him before his surgery.

As I wrote in Chapter 5, in 2011 I had a serious fall in our home, when I came inside with snow on my shoes and fell flat on my face in our front hall. I broke the tibial plateau on my left knee, the part of the knee that the femur rests on which allows the knee to bend. As well, I broke both bones in my right wrist from trying to break my fall, I had a black eye, and only by the grace of God did I miss hitting the newel post on our stairway. It could have been so much worse than it was. Initially I didn't realize how badly I was hurt, and

I kept saying, "Just let me lie here for a little while. I'm okay." I was not afraid at all; on the contrary, I was very calm. After about fifteen minutes my husband realized I wasn't going to be able to get up and called the EMTs.

Even though I was severely injured, to the point that I nearly died twice in the hospital, I always felt taken care of and unafraid. I knew everything would be all right. For some reason, I totally trusted that God was taking care of me and that I had nothing to fear. Maybe that was the Percocet talking, but I certainly was not afraid.

In this case, it was my husband who had to hold the space for me. He couldn't do anything for me other than to sit by my bedside in the ER and make sure I was comfortable. He could ask the nurses for an extra blanket or some water, but otherwise, he had to trust that all would be okay. It was much harder for him than it was for me.

Any time we have to hold the space for someone we love, it is a burden on us. It can be when a dearly loved child is on drugs, or we lose our job, or our home to a flood, a forest fire or a tornado. Perhaps it will turn out to be a dear friend who suddenly loses her husband of forty years and can't make sense of his passing.

How do you cope with sudden loss? How do you move on, into this new normal that has become your life?

It can be done only one moment at a time. Sometimes we have to hold the space for ourselves in order to find that new way of being, that new wisdom we really didn't want to have to acquire with so much pain.

I have a dear friend who lost her husband last year. She lives in an isolated area, away from family and friends, because her husband had wanted to move to a home with acreage. Since her friends still live in her previous city, she has had to learn to do this most difficult task on her own. Some days, she says, it's all she can do to just sit on the couch and tell herself over and over to breathe. In and out, in and out. It's how she copes.

We have to allow ourselves this space, so that we can heal and finally find the new person we are becoming.

I have often thought it really strange that some of the most difficult lessons we have to learn come at the highest expense. Wouldn't it be nice if we could just magically have all this new wisdom, all these great insights, without having to go through the devastation that is required in order for the learning to take place?

But that's not how it works. And maybe that's the whole point. We're not supposed to get it all at once; it's a process that we must go through to learn whatever we need to learn to grow from our times of trial.

Jesus shows us so clearly that the crucifixion has to come before the Resurrection. Then and only then can He be transformed into His new self, so different from His old way of being that even His dear friend Mary Magdalene didn't recognize Him on Easter morning.

And speaking of that awful event that is at the center of our faith, how must Mary, the mother of Jesus, Mary Magdalene, and the Apostle John have felt while they were watching Jesus go through the long process of dying? I often wonder if Mary didn't think to herself, "Surely God will work a miracle, and Jesus will be released from the cross without actually dying. Won't He? He has done so many miracles in my life, surely God will be merciful and work one more."

But we know that's not what happened at all. She had to hold the space for Jesus to die. Mary must have been tempted, though. She probably didn't want to go through her own suffering any more than you or I do. It's too hard; we feel as though we can't do it. But somehow we do, and perhaps many months or a year later, we find we are moving on. We did get through it, and no, it wasn't easy.

From our perspective of two thousand years later we know that Jesus had to endure His death and become transformed in order to show us that this transformation is possible for us as well. So often what is required of us is just to stand still and let the new way of being wash over us, sort of like a new kind of baptism, our own resurrection into new life.

It ain't easy.

One of the things I discovered in my journey back to wholeness after my fall, though, is that even with the pain, there are very often enormous gifts that show up.

The consequence of my fall was that I needed to be in a rehab facility for about seven weeks after I left the hospital the day after Christmas. I had never been in such a place, never had to be dependent on someone to do even the slightest, most disgusting things that I could not do for myself. One of the most immediate gifts was that the CNAs (Certified Nurse's Assistants) all were so unfailingly kind and that they handled all the grunt work with the greatest good cheer. They were truly God's special angels.

One day I remarked to one of them that I was very impressed with the way they were all so loving. She replied, "Well, I just imagine that every patient is my grandmother or my grandfather. I treat them the same way that I would want them to be treated."

What a lovely attitude of service!

It was not until many months had passed that I understood the purpose behind this whole episode and the gift that truly showed up.

As I described in Chapter 5, my parish family for nearly thirty-five years, got a new, dictatorial priest. Very soon, people started leaving in droves. I was one of them.

It was a time of deep grieving for me and for many others, as we suddenly found ourselves adrift without our usual church home and friends. It was almost like a death in the family.

I had started going to another Catholic church, but it didn't really feel like a good fit for me, either. In fact, many of my friends joked that we had become "Roamin' Catholics," because we tried one parish after another, hoping to recreate what we had had before in our old church home. We felt adrift, both spiritually and emotionally. It was horrible, a real "dark night of the soul" experience.

My wise and loving friend Pat is a very positive person who always looks for the gift in any situation. As she always counsels me, "Look beyond the physical circumstances to see where Source may be leading you to go next."

One result of my fall was that I was unable to go to Mass *anywhere* for six months, which gave me a great deal of time to discern exactly what I would be looking for in a parish once I was well enough to walk again. It was as if God had understood my frustration with the present situation and had given me the gift of time to figure it out.

Often God knows we want to change something in our lives that isn't working, but we lack the courage to make an adjustment until we are forced to find a new way of looking at things. Sometimes when we need to make such a shift, we find ourselves in a situation that has us confused and feeling lost, and we need a process of discernment to decide what the new thing should be and how best to go about getting it. Unless we are compelled by circumstances that are so uncomfortable that we have to do something about them, we usually will not take the necessary steps to make the alteration that we need to make.

I once heard a story about climate change that seems to illustrate this situation exactly, even though at first glance the two sets of circumstances could not be more different. I don't know if this was about a real event or if the teller of the tale was simply using it to make a point, but it can certainly be used as a teaching parable in either case.

Because the sea was rising very quickly in Alaska, many sea mammals, polar bears, seals, and others were trapped when an ice dam cut off their normal access to the deep ocean. They found themselves in a sort of lake which had sea water but no direct access to their regular feeding grounds. This state of affairs also meant that they were cut off from their regular prey, and many animals began to die off.

However, before there was complete annihilation of the bears and the seals, the pressure on the newly formed dam became so great that all at once the entire thing collapsed, and the animals were once again able to feed in the larger ocean. The situation had resolved itself of its own accord because the pressure was too great for it not to occur.

In my case, when the pressure for all of us who were searching for something else grew to be too great, the dam burst in a way we could not have anticipated. We were not even necessarily conscious that that was what was happening, but the end result was the same. We were forced to give up our old habits and ways for the sake of growing larger and more expansive. I was handed this wonderful gift of time, and it has turned out to have been the perfect thing for me. As I have talked with others who shared this experience of losing our beloved church home, we have all come to realize that it has been a great gift, even though it was in disguise at the time.

Another part of this wonderful gift that showed up for me was that of having the time to meditate for many hours, especially in the deepest, darkest part of the night when everything was still. I found it a precious time to be with God, or with Mother Mary.

I have never had a particularly close relationship with Mary, finding her generally too sanitized, too formal, like the statues we had in our church, to be a good role model. There she was in her beautiful blue robes, looking saintly, with her arms outstretched. She never seemed to me to be a real person, like one who would get her hands dirty with real life. But for some reason, while I was in rehab, I often found myself calling on her to help with my healing.

The Mary I encountered then was not at all the pristine, clean plaster saint clad all in blue that I was used to seeing. No, this Mary was different. This Mary was a woman of the earth, dressed in a deep red skirt and white peasant blouse, with her dark hair in a braid that reached to her waist. She was barefoot, and she didn't mind at all getting her hands dirty as she sat on the floor by my bed and gently kneaded the muscles around my knee. She was gentle, and her whole being was concentrated on my healing.

Whenever I would break down in despair, thinking that my knee was never going to heal, she would always remind me that things were perfectly on schedule, exactly as they should be, and to let go and let the process do what needed to be done.

My new mantra became, "Let it be; let it go." I learned to trust that Mary would be there to hold the space for me while I healed.

I found myself singing the old Beatles' song, "Let It Be" over and over to myself. It was hugely calming, as was Mary's presence. I don't know if she was really there or if she was only a figment of my imagination. In the end, it probably doesn't matter. What was important then was that I felt her as a healing presence, and the wisdom to "Let go and let it be" was as vital as any medicine for me.

The lesson once again was to surrender and to let God handle the details. Such a hard lesson for someone like me who was raised to be proudly independent! It was probably the most important gift from the whole experience.

Perhaps you yourself have had a similar time in your life when you were forced to learn to step back and do nothing, because there was nothing you *could* do. You had to learn to surrender in order to move forward. It's not a lesson we want to learn.

The point of this story is about being ready to face whatever we are called to face in our lives, whether it is our own experience or listening to the experience of someone else.

When we are listening with compassion to another's story, we are holding the space for them to try to heal whatever has happened. We are thus able to bring grace into the moment and to help make it a sacred sharing. When we turn someone away without fully listening to them, we deprive both ourselves and the other person of a chance to partake in the graced moment. It can become a blessing for both of us if we let it.

My fall finally allowed me to understand more of what the Church means when we talk about the Mystical Body of Christ. We are all energetic beings as well as physical bodies. In this way we are truly connected to all the other beings on the planet, because we all have this energetic signature.

The message that we are all fundamentally one at our essence is not new, and it is certainly not unique to the Catholic Church. Many religions speak of the oneness of all beings.

Several years ago Deepak Chopra gave a lecture to a group of people in my town. Dr. Chopra, as you may know, is a well-known scientist who runs The Chopra Center for Wellbeing in Carlsbad, California. He is also a renowned physician with a background in internal medicine and endocrinology, as well as being a spiritual healer who has written eighty books. He's a very inspirational speaker who comes from a very deep soul place inside himself. What he says resonates with huge numbers of people all around the world.

He made the point that all of us are connected by the very air that we breathe, since the molecules of air that we exhale are then breathed in by anyone who is in the same room with us. Think of being in a large crowd, all of the people breathing, in and out, in and out, taking in one another's' breaths with every inhalation, and breathing out our own and everyone else's breaths when we breathe out. We actually end up by exchanging one another's genetic material at the same time. How's that for a mind-blowing thought?

When we come to the realization that the Holy Spirit is breath—spirit means breath, after all—that S/he is breathing not only you but all of that huge gathering of people, then the idea of all of us being the cosmic Body of Christ doesn't seem so far-fetched at all.

Chopra goes even further when he says that all of us are still breathing in dust from the Big Bang, which occurred four billion years ago. Mind-blowing, indeed. I have since heard this same concept enunciated by other teachers, including Rick Stein, who teaches in a monastery outside of Colorado Springs. He was teaching a four-part series to our adult education class about Teilhard de Chardin, a French Jesuit (1881-1953) who also had this same belief. So perhaps it's not as far out as I first had imagined it to be.

Somehow the idea that we are all one suddenly makes a lot of sense. It's not just a "woo-woo" New Age-y concept anymore but scientific reality.

If this insight is true, and I think it is, then how is it that we continue to treat each other so badly? How does war—any war—make sense? How does killing innocent men, women, and children who have done nothing more than to be born with the "wrong" color skin, or to worship God in a different manner from some other group seem like such a good idea to so many? Don't we understand yet that God who is all about Love doesn't do "wrong?" We are all made in His image and likeness, so we can't be somehow "wrong."

If we truly are all one, are we not just fighting with another part of our own selves?

Recently it has seemed that bullying each other is the new way of relating with one another. Whether it is kids taunting their classmates for being too different or political candidates spewing venom at each other, we apparently don't recognize that this other person is a human being who is worthy of respect and dignity just because they are also humans.

If we are trying to teach children to be respectful of one another at school, what kind of message does it send when someone insults another person on the Internet and gets hundreds of "likes?" Children learn by watching how adults treat one another, after all.

There was a news report in May 2016 about an attack that happened at a convention of two rival bicycle gangs in Denver. One of the members shot another who was of the opposing gang for using the "wrong staircase" in the building where the meeting was being held. It seems that the first group had a commercial booth set up by "their" staircase, which the other group was daring to use, even though this was a public building open to all. The killer decided that no one other than members of his own gang had the right to use those stairs, and that it gave him a perfect reason to shoot and kill another person.

It seems to me that we would all be more peaceful inside if we didn't appoint ourselves to be the supreme arbiters of everyone else's life, if we would allow ourselves and everyone else the space to find their own way to the Love that made the universe. I want to be able to stand still and hold that sacred space, both for myself and for other people.

Standing still is often not an easy thing to do, especially in our hurry-up world that demands that we move ever faster and more frantically, trying to get more done with less sleep, less time to ourselves to wonder about the world and what we actually think about what we want from life. I think it is imperative that we make the time to slow down and allow ourselves to be in the moment, because ultimately that is where we will find God, and in discovering the divine spark within us we will finally be able to know who we really are. We have to make time in our everyday life to give our sacred self the great gift of showing us why we are here on earth.

CHAPTER 7

Standing in Darkness

As much as we talk about "living in the Light" and being "People of the Light," I think we do ourselves a disservice not to recognize the power of darkness.

Even our language is geared to make darkness or shadows to be "the bad guy." Think about it. The good guys wear white hats; the bad guys wear black. Darkness is often seen as evil, or at least where evil lurks, ready to pounce on us unawares.

I wouldn't be surprised to find out that our fear of the dark, of the scary boogeymen that hide under our beds as children, is at the basis for much of our racism. After all, many people grew up distrusting those people who have darker skin than they do. While the racism may be subliminal and not at all on the surface, it still may have its roots in our language and cultural ideas of blackness as being somehow bad. It may also have something to do with not being able to see well in the dark. I have no scientific evidence for this idea, but it does make me wonder.

And yet, there is another side to darkness, the deep cocoon we drop into during the nighttime hours when we sleep and dream, or the mystical place we go to in our meditations, which may also feel like darkness. But this type of darkness has within it a sense of renewal, of new life springing up, much like the seeds that lie dormant during wintertime, hiding underground until the time is right for the shoots to spring up and become the flowers of spring.

Darkness is as necessary to us as is the light. In fact, without darkness, we would have no concept whatsoever of light. We need the contrast to be able to see one or the other. If everything is the same, how can we possibly tell which is which? This concept holds true for any two things that we perceive as being opposites. We must have both in order to decide which attribute or item we want to pursue at a given time.

This is not to say that one thing is better than another, or more perfect, or more desirable. On the contrary, we need both good *and* bad, high *and* low, in *and* out, cold *and* hot in order to decide which of the two we want to choose in a particular instance. This dualistic way of looking at things happens in every aspect of our lives, from preferring to live near the mountains rather than on the plains, or liking rivers and lakes more than we like the ocean. We can certainly agree that everyone has preferences in food or drink.

The same thing is true when it comes to darkness and light. Some people are night owls because they come alive after dark, while others are robins or finches who love the early morning. One thing is not better than another. It is a matter of personal choice.

However, for some reason, when we hear the term "darkness" as it relates to spirituality, our minds almost automatically shift into, "Oh, no! Not the darkness! Anything but that!" And yet the darkness holds untold riches for those who choose to allow that scary place in their consciousness.

The movie *Into the Woods*, the marvelous Stephen Sondheim musical, is a retelling of several of the Grimm's fairytales—with a twist. Nothing goes like it does in the stories. Cinderella gets the Prince, all right, but then he turns out to be unfaithful to her. Not what she had had in mind at all.

Little Red Riding Hood is so sure she can handle whatever she finds in the woods on the way to Granny's house, that she sets off happily, only to be set upon and lured by the wicked Wolf.

As I watched this clever retelling of the stories I couldn't help but think that the woods are the metaphor for all that is deep and dark and scary within each one of us. As many psychologists and spiritual writers from Carl Jung to Brandon Bays, Kevin Billett, Gangaji, and others know, we all must end up going "into the woods" and facing whatever lurks there to snare and derail us in our lives. How we choose to deal with the dark parts of ourselves, what Debbie Ford called the "shadow side," ultimately determines whether or not we survive our encounter with life itself, or at the very least, how well we cope with all those events in our lives that bring us to our knees.

Going into the forest can be scary. Since I live in Colorado I am always hearing on TV or reading a news story about someone who has gone hiking in our mountains and gotten lost. It's easy to miss a poorly marked rock cairn or miss a blaze marker high on a tree on the trail, and very often the person or family must spend a very dark night in a cold, scary place without enough food or water. So using the deep woods as a metaphor for our own interior darkness doesn't seem strange to me at all. People do die from exposure sometimes in these cases, and at best they may be found, tired, hungry, and frightened after a bad night.

I know that some people are so afraid of facing their own inner demons that they find solace in the bottle, or drugs, or may even be driven to suicide because those choices are more palatable than dealing with whatever they fear is within themselves. They may have to lose all that is precious to them—their homes, their jobs, their families—before they finally hit bottom and decide to change the way they live.

This is the time then that meditation and prayer can truly be life savers.

But first a caveat: What if we hit something so dark and dangerous-feeling when we are meditating that we don't know how to handle it? Well, if it is so painful that you don't know how to handle it, I would suggest seeing someone who is trained as a therapist to help you. Meditation may not be the right approach for you at this time.

There is, however, another idea that may also aid in your search for your true self.

Just as there are many ways to solve a particular problem, there are also different ways to approach God. Some of these may be familiar to you; others, not so much.

First, there is the usual way most of us learn about God, which is called the *via positiva,* or the positive way of looking at God. This is the way many Christians first were taught about who God is: He is loving and kind, He is all-powerful, He created the world and all that is in it, He is part of the Holy Trinity, Father, Son, and Spirit, or whatever your faith tradition sets forth as the way things are. These attributes are about what the Deity is like, the more or less obvious things that many people take for granted.

If you are not Christian but instead you identify with another religion, then your images of God, or Allah, or Shiva may be different. You may call that Higher Power the One, or the Living Light, or Yahweh. That's okay. All roads will lead eventually to the same place, the same ultimate reality, regardless of the way your tradition teaches you to envision the One Who is All-in-All. This is called the Perennial Philosophy, because it transcends all traditions and time periods. The *via positiva* still applies to your belief system, because it describes the normal way any faith tradition thinks of Source, or the picture we have of Him/Her/It/Them.

There is a second way, called the *via negativa*, which is about the things that God is not. He has no gender, He has no body or human attributes, He is everywhere and nowhere in particular at the same time, He is not a created being like we are, so therefore He is no thing. He is not even "He." He is just pure being. We only name

Him "He" because we have to call the Eternal One by some term so that we can talk about the Deity.

Pure being is the way God appears to us when we are truly in a state of union with Him. We cannot see Him, or feel Him, or touch, taste, or smell Him, but we are aware of *something*, a Presence that we call God. You may have a different name for the Divine Presence than God, which is a fraught term for many people. The name is not as important as the concept. No one really knows what God calls Him/Her/It/Themselves. For most people it is hard to even think about such things. Our minds just go around and around getting nowhere.

The third way of relating to God is the *via creativa,* or the creative way of looking at God. We have access to this way of finding God whenever we are creative in any way. For artists, musicians, actors, and those who make things out of nothing, the *via creativa* is the normal way of relating to God. Seeing God in the beauty of a sunset or a snow-covered mountain may also come under this category.

Many people don't think that they are creative, but they are, although probably a large percentage of the population has never thought about relating to God in this way. It only takes a slightly different way of looking at what we define as being creative to find the many ways that each of us is creative every day. We may see God in a lovely painting, or feel His presence in a sublime piece of music. He may be all around us in the things we see in nature: a glorious sunset, a beautiful flower or tree, a perfect seashell. Perhaps we feel drawn to try to write a poem about the wonders of God's creation, or to spend a day feeling the majesty of the mountains as we toil towards the summit. Some people may feel close to eternity when they hold a child or a beloved pet, or design the perfect house or garden, or cook a delicious meal from scratch.

The union between what happens in the *via negativa* and the *via creativa* is the birth of real wisdom, which of course is also where we find God in many religious traditions. The wisdom that is meant here is *Sophia,* which is another name for the Holy Spirit. Since *Sophia* is a feminine name, at least in Latin-based languages, some people see the Holy Spirit as representing the divine female principle that contains the totality of God along with God the Father. However, that only works in some languages; certainly not all tongues equate wisdom with women.

Be that as it may, there are many creative ways to God. Mozart and Bach, the sublime composers, certainly understood how to find God in the creative way, as did Michelangelo and Da Vinci in art. Those who live the creative way may be from any field of endeavor, such as the sciences, cooking, or industry. Those who come up with ideas for new products are certainly living from the way of creativity.

You may be a creative teacher, or an astronaut. You may find ways to make creative and innovative dishes to put on your family's table each night. You may design and make beautiful clothing for yourself or others, either as a hobby or as a business. You may see the elegant beauty of a mathematic equation, or design airplanes, such as the plane that recently flew around the world powered only by solar energy. Think what a revolution in energy use this development may trigger! Who is to say that that is not creative work? You may think of other ways that are especially meaningful to you.

The fourth and last category of experiencing God is called the *via transformativa.* This is the area in which all the other aspects of the ways we worship come together. How does all of this transform our lives? Are we called to be people who spend weekends feeding the hungry at a soup kitchen? Do we donate clothing and food to homeless shelters? Do we volunteer to take meals to shut-ins? What are the special ways we thank God for all that we have received? Are we living life so as to be close to God in everything we do each and every day? Do we love God as well as the people we meet?

There are as many ways for us to transform our world as there are people in it. We each have our own special set of talents and gifts that only we can give to the world. Maybe yours is teaching children to read, or being a nurse or a physician who heals the physical ills of those who are in need. You could be an inspirational movie director, or an actor, or a singer, or a comedian who lifts the spirits of those who see the show. One of my cousins is very talented as a negotiator, and she helps to bring peace to those who find themselves at odds over land and resources. Others are good with languages, fixing cars, landscape artists, and computer experts.

Only you know what your special area of expertise is. Any profession or talent can be a way to help us to draw closer to God; it is the *attitude* that makes the difference. It doesn't really matter if one is a janitor or the president of a company worth billions. How we approach our job is the important thing. It feels very different if we are just in it for the money, or if instead we believe that we are contributing to the community as a whole.

There is an old story about a man who came upon three others who were chopping big blocks of stone out of boulders. The first man asked what they were doing.

"I am chopping up this huge stone into smaller pieces," said the first, mopping the sweat from his face.

"I am working to support my family," the second one replied in a bored voice. "It pays the bills."

"Me?" responded the third man. "Why, I am building a great cathedral for the honor and glory of God." His face shone with joy.

I have no idea where I first heard that tale, but it illustrates perfectly how important our attitude is. Each answered the question according to his own beliefs, but how each man felt about himself and his work made the job either just something to do to get through the day, or it gave him a sense of dignity and purpose.

I want to spend some time now with the *via negativa,* since this chapter is about standing in darkness, especially as it relates to meditation.

One of the best books on meditation is by an anonymous monk of the fourteenth century, who was writing for the cloistered monks he knew. We can only surmise who he was, since he didn't attach his name to his writings. Nevertheless, his work has survived for all these intervening centuries, and it is prized by those who are serious about using meditation as a way to get closer to God. It seems as though he must have been a novice master in a monastery of some kind, for he refers to the "young men" who think they know everything, when really they know very little.

There are many translations of *The Cloud of Unknowing,* which is the way he refers to what he calls the "prayer of quiet," or what we now call Centering Prayer, the meditation method popularized by Father Thomas Keating, the Cistercian monk who now resides at the Abbey of St. Benedict in Snowmass, Colorado.

Some of the translations of *The Cloud* are obscure and difficult to read; I like the one by Carmen Acevedo Butcher, published by Shambala Publications, Inc. There are dozens of translations of this book; Amazon had about fifteen or more for sale when I was looking on their site. Butcher is an associate professor of English at Shorter College in Rome, Georgia who has written extensively on Christian mystics, including her books *A Life of Saint Benedict* and *Hildegard of Bingen: A Spiritual Reader.* Butcher writes in a loose, contemporary English style which is easy to understand. It is a difficult subject, but she makes it very accessible.

The 14th Century author of *The Cloud,* whom we will call Anonymous, is very careful to state what can and cannot be accomplished by meditation. He assures his readers that there will always be a darkness, a "Cloud of Unknowing" between themselves and God. They will not be suddenly enlightened by knowing everything there is to know about God just because they have begun to meditate. They will have to get used to being in the darkness. The mystery of God will not magically reveal itself in their interior prayer. However, they should not let the darkness deter them from seeking God. Their intellect is simply not capable of knowing Him completely, and that is all right. That is not their job, anyway. Their job is to seek Him sincerely, with a loving heart, and to rejoice in being in His presence.

In this respect, Anonymous sounds a whole lot like Father Thomas Keating and the way he describes Centering Prayer. Again, the intention to be with God should be the primary focus of meditation. Never mind that chattering "monkey mind" that we all have; it just goes with the territory. The intellect will never get us closer to God; only love can do that. Even though we try and try to "think our way to God," we find only that we get farther and farther away the more earnestly we try, and we are left not knowing more than we do know.

It's a bit like that optical illusion that shows two different images. Do we see the faces on the sides of the picture? Or do we see the urn in the center? It all depends upon our perspective, and if we gaze at the picture long enough, we will see first one and then the other if we let our vision blur. Each part of the picture is based on the negative space surrounding the other image. The harder we concentrate, the less we see. We must let our focus go soft and not try to "make something happen."

Anonymous says that's true of prayer as well. We must make it our intention to spend time with God and then leave the rest of it up to Her. Nobody ever finds God through willpower alone. Grace must enter into the equation as well. Father Keating refers to this aspect of Centering as giving our consent to spend time with God, and then letting Him take care of the details.

The second book that is included with *The Cloud of Unknowing*, at least in Butcher's translation, is *The Book of Privy Counsel*, which seems to be a book for more advanced students of meditation.

Anonymous perhaps wrote it somewhat later than the earlier book, maybe after he had been training novices for a while and realized that some of them were starting to get beyond the beginner stage.

In any case, apparently some of his students were questioning if meditation was really the right practice for them. Anonymous replies that only God can call a person to this type of prayer, and here are some of the signs by which you will know if it is for you.

Usually those who really feel the hunger and thirst for the Holy One find themselves drawn to meditation. Other types of praying just don't satisfy their hearts. However, sometimes we like *the idea* of meditation more than we enjoy the actual sitting still, which is not always an easy thing to do.

Our bodies may suddenly develop aches and pains that we have never noticed until we began to try to sit in one position for twenty or thirty minutes. We may have to cough or sneeze, or perhaps we become very sleepy. Do these things mean that we should not go for a meditative practice? Not necessarily.

Often when we experience these minor (or possibly not so minor!) annoyances we think that maybe we aren't cut out for this type of prayer. If these things happen often, then we can try taking a break from meditating every day, and see how we feel without contemplative life. If we think, "Whew! Am I glad that's over!" then maybe we really are not ready for the discipline meditation entails.

But if instead we find ourselves to be longing for the intimate union that we feel when we have a sitting practice, then we owe it to ourselves to give meditation a second look. Sometimes people come at contemplation before they are really ready to commit to it, or they don't really understand exactly what having such a practice entails. That's okay. It is much like any other field of endeavor that requires practice and sticking with it.

Imagine a child who is starting to learn to play the piano. At first, it may be exciting to hear sounds that he makes by striking the keys, but after a few lessons, he realizes that he is going to have to practice every day in order to make progress. Now that is a very different enterprise. It can be boring to sit and play scales day after day, constantly making mistakes and feeling like there is no progress. But when he commits to the practice, very soon he is making real music, and he understands that the scales help his hands know where they should be on the keys. At that point, the beauty of the music itself, and his joy in accomplishing a difficult task make the whole thing worthwhile.

Meditation can be like that, too. Sometimes we would rather be anywhere else than sitting still and contemplating. Initially we may find ourselves very excited to try to reach God in this sustained way. However, perhaps after a few weeks it becomes nothing but a grind, and we feel like the piano student that we are not getting anywhere.

That is where the discipline comes in. If we can just keep at it, eventually we find that it becomes easier and easier to come to contemplation, and that even when we feel like nothing is happening, God is still present in our breath and our life.

One of the problems that can occur is that we become attuned to the sounds all around us. Our world can be very noisy, from birdsong and the din of construction outside our window, to children playing in the house or out in the yard. We have to be able to hear these things without paying attention to them. That can be difficult, if not downright impossible.

I remember being in a class about meditation many years ago, and the instruction was to keep our attention on our breath no matter what else was going on in the room. Several of the assistants came in banging on pots and pans, which they held right next to our heads. Others dropped silverware on us, while still others shot water pistols at us. People were singing loudly into our ears while some had conversations that erupted into raucous laughter. Not so easy to keep one's focus with all of that nonsense going on!

Now whenever I am meditating and I hear the crazy mourning dove who sounds like he's on steroids, or my cat starts yowling at my feet, I have to remind myself to let it all go and just be present to the breath.

If, however, one decides that meditation is not for her, or at least, not at this time, that is okay, too. Not everyone is called to become a mystic. Perhaps our talents and desires lie in a different direction. God is like that. He calls everyone to the things that make the most sense for them spiritually. Not all of us are the same in that respect. And isn't that a good thing? God always gives us a choice about how to relate to Him.

One difficulty that arises in meditation is that we always, *always* have the darkness of not really knowing who and what God is. We may think we do, especially if we belong to a religious congregation, but the reality is that God Himself is constantly hidden from us. It is up to us to learn to be okay with the "not knowing," because that is all that we are going to get in this life.

What we *do* finally come to realize when we meditate is that God is always present. Often we will become aware of a Presence around us, but that is a consolation that is not always available to our conscious mind. So we are literally standing in the dark most of the time, and most of us have trouble with ambiguity.

Perhaps that is why some people are more comfortable beginning their practice with guided meditation, which gives them something tangible to imagine or to focus on. Guided meditations may lead the listener to a special place such as a lake, a mountain, or a beautiful home that they design in their minds. They may be led into a cave, or into outer space, where they must solve a problem, or discover something about themselves that they hadn't known before. This is a much easier way for the person to enter into stillness and yet have something for the restless "monkey mind" to do.

Eventually, however, even that is not enough for the one who desires to be only with God, not with some imaginary or human-made environment. When we come to that place, then we know we are really ready for Centering Prayer-type contemplation, because we are not focused on anything in Scripture or the imagination; we are ready for the darkness of not knowing. Our notion of who God is has changed.

I was talking to a friend of mine recently who had left one religion for another, explaining that the version of God she was being exposed to in her previous church was "just too small." She had evolved to the place where her idea of who God is had expanded to include everyone, all the planets, all the solar systems, and all the galaxies. Anything less was not large enough to contain her God. I understood exactly what she meant, because the word "God" means different things to each of us.

So now. How should we go about our prayer life outside of our meditation times? What things are appropriate to say to God? I talk to God exactly as I would talk to my best friend. There is nothing off limits. He has heard it all before. I am sure I won't shock Him, or make Him hate me, or anything along those lines. He is much bigger than that.

If I am angry, even with Him, then I say so. I want to get it off my chest. If I need something, I ask for it. If I am scared about what is happening with someone in my family, or if I don't know how to deal with a situation, I tell Him so. Just the act of getting it out of my system makes me feel better and calm down, and then I am able to see the issue more clearly. At that point, what I usually feel is a great sense of relief and gratitude. Then I can thank God and be sincere about it, because the relationship is based on honesty.

Earlier I mentioned the great 13th century mystic, Julian of Norwich, and her saying about how things will always be well with God's help. At first when I read her book, *Showings,* which is about a series of visions she received from God over a day and a half period, I thought, She's crazy. So many things are wrong with our world! How can Julian say that all will be well?

The more I thought about that statement and prayed about it, I began to understand what she was talking about.

There is an old story that goes something like this:

Once there was a poor old farmer who had one son. The son helped him to plow the fields, but it was slow going and very tiring. So the farmer saved his money to buy a horse. That was good. The horse helped the two of them to plow the fields much more easily.

But the son was out one day riding the horse when he got thrown off and broke his leg. This was very bad, because now who would help the farmer to do his plowing?

The next day, some soldiers showed up looking for young men to join the army. Ooh, bad.

But the son had a broken leg, so he couldn't go. Ah, that was good!

This story can go on and on, with something being at first good, then terrible, then good again, and eventually God brings some good out of every situation. Oh. I get it. "All will be well, and all will be well, and all manner of things will be well." Maybe just not right away, but eventually, all *will* be well. If we really trust that things will at some point get better, it only makes sense that we ask God for assistance with the mundane things of our lives, which brings us to why and how we pray, and what things we are likely to pray for.

"Help," the word we use most often, is what the Church refers to as *a prayer of petition*. When we find ourselves in places or situations we realize we just can't deal with alone, that's the time we turn to God for assistance. A family member is sick, we have lost our job, our house, or our spouse, and we are drowning. The only word that comes to us to say is, "Help me. Help! HELP!! I can't do this anymore. I don't know who else to turn to. Help!"

However, asking for help is not limited to the big things. We turn to God with our prayers for the small concerns, as well. "Help me pass my math test tomorrow. Help me find a parking place that isn't too far away from the doctor's office. Please give me the courage to say the right thing to the friend that I've hurt." We say this kind of prayer almost automatically, especially if we have been taught to ask God for what we need. We trust that Source will show us the way.

The Mass has a section that is called "The Prayers of the Faithful," in which we pray for the leaders of our country, the sick, those in war-torn lands, and other petitions. In addition, I belong to two different prayer chains. These loosely-knit groups pray for the intentions of anyone who asks them for help. Usually these burdens are things like, "Help me find a job so I can pay the rent this month. Help me buy a car so that I can get to work on time every day. My daughter is sick and in the hospital awaiting the results of tests. Help her to get well soon."

If the prayer is for something really big, like the death of someone we love, even in such cases eventually we begin to realize, "Hey, I'm moving on. I'm still alive. The sun is still shining, day after day. I am still breathing, one breath at a time. Maybe I *can* make it after all. Thanks, God. Thank You, thank You. I think I'm going to be all right." Now the situation may or may not have resolved itself; we may still be without the house and the things that burned up in a fire or were lost in a flood, yet we have somehow come to terms with our loss or changed circumstances. The sick family member may have gotten better, but perhaps not. Maybe we have had to face a death. In any case, *we* have changed, which brings us to the third stage, "Wow. That was amazing. *You* are amazing, God. Thanks. Wow!"

So far we have talked about the *prayer of petition*, or asking God for a favor, and the *prayer of thanksgiving*. There is also the *prayer of adoration*, or giving glory to God as the angels did in Bethlehem at Jesus' birth: "Glory to God in the highest, and on earth, peace to people of good will." In the Book of Job in the Old Testament, the author says in Chapter 37: 14, "Hearken to this, O Job! Stand and consider the wondrous works of God!"

Giving glory and praise to God seems to be an especially meaningful way of thanking Her for big things, such as winning a war, or having a favorable harvest. People use this prayer when just an ordinary thank you doesn't seem to be enough, because they recognize that it takes a Supreme Being to make these things happen: rain after a drought, fair winds when one is sailing the seas, a miracle of healing an incurable cancer.

The next kind of prayer, though, is a bit different. It is the *prayer of atonement*, in which we ask forgiveness for a wrong that we have done to someone else: "Please forgive me for the way I treated my friend at school today. That was a dumb thing to say, and it hurt her." "I stole some money from my mom's purse. Please forgive me." In these examples it would serve us well also to ask forgiveness from the person we have hurt. An attitude of resolve not to do these types of things again is also helpful.

There are two transformational ways to God, suffering and great love. These paths to the Almighty are not exactly prayers, but they are prayerful means of growing in the spiritual life.

Suffering, or standing in darkness, always is about our need for God to help us get through some experience that is unpleasant or uncomfortable. Paradoxically, those times seem to be the times when we grow the most because it is too unpleasant to stay where we are. We would never make progress otherwise. Why would we change if everything is perfect? There would be no need. Our very evolution as people and as a species is based on the idea that we will try to change things when they are too unbearable to keep on keeping on.

Psychologists often say that the very definition of insanity is to keep doing the same old things and expecting to get different results. If it works, great, but if we find ourselves mired in the muck and we can't get out, that's when we turn to God. "Help me. Please. Please help me. I am stuck, and I can't do this by myself."

That's when we learn to do things differently. I find that I pray this kind of prayer a lot.

The second way to transformation is through great love, which causes us to do all kinds of things that we would never have otherwise dreamed we would do. This is the kind of love that allows us to sit for hours at the bedside of a seriously ill child, spouse, or parent without worrying what time it is. It never crosses our mind whether or not we'll make it to the movie on time, because seeing a movie is suddenly not important to us at all. Nothing in the world is more important than to be with our loved one. There is nowhere else we would rather be than right where we are.

Love of God is that way, too. Our desire is to spend time with the Beloved in silence, or to go to Mass every Sunday if we are Catholic, not because it's required but because we want to be there. There is nowhere else we would rather be, in fact. Obligation doesn't enter into it for a moment.

Prayer is one way of learning how to be with great love or great suffering throughout our lives. We must get our own Ego out of the way so that God has room to enter in. This is what St. John is talking about when he says, "Unless a grain of wheat dies, it remains a single grain. But if it dies, it will yield a great harvest." The grain that dies becomes wheat that is much bigger than the little seed it once was.

Meditation seems to be an especially wonderful way to achieve taming our Ego and getting it to do what it is good for, namely helping us to function in the world around us. It is only when we start to think that only we know how to proceed in the spiritual life that it becomes a problem. In fact, the more we meditate, the more we realize how little we actually do know, and thus it helps if we can approach the silence with the attitude of having a beginner's mind. We soon begin to understand that we must rely on the Spirit to show us how to proceed if we truly are serious about making progress in the spiritual life.

While it doesn't really make any difference as to what time of day to meditate, some hours seem to be more fruitful than others, even though we can profit from sitting still at any hour. Each period has its own special quality, and all parts of the day contain unique and wonderful experiences. That being said, there is something I especially like about the sacred nighttime hours, which feel unfathomable and filled with awe.

I have not yet talked about the quality of darkness itself and what the absence of light feels like. When I was a child we often went to church at night when it was dark, especially during Lent when it was often also still very cold and sometimes snowy or damp and dreary. Our parish didn't have enough money to heat the church for the Stations of the Cross or Benediction, so we would all sit there in our heavy coats, scarves, mittens and boots, freezing in addition to being without much light.

I am sure it was uncomfortable at best, but my memories of those times are more about the mystery than about the discomfort. There is something special about being in a dark place that we usually only see in the daylight. It could have been a bit scary to see the shadowy statues and the shapes of things without light that would seem perfectly ordinary in the daytime. At night those same familiar things in the dimness might look like monsters or evil beasts, although I don't really remember being afraid. My trust in God was so absolute that I just knew He would take care of me, especially since I was in His house.

What I know about darkness is how sacred it feels. The absence of light bestows a totally different quality than what is felt during the daytime. Since God is Mystery even in bright sunlight, how much more that delicious feeling of being deep within the spaciousness of God Himself is when there is little light other than the tiny red flame of the candle that always burns in the sanctuary. It is that blessed feeling of quiet and peace, eternal and deep. It is the feeling of holiness itself.

I loved—still love—that feeling. It is like being held in the arms of the Eternal One, huge and majestic while at the same time being comforted and beloved.

I can certainly understand why the ancient monasteries and convents began their Liturgy of the Hours in the wee hours of the morning. Imagine being with Hildegard in her early convent at Disibodenberg in the Rhine Valley in Germany on a cold, rainy November night. You are awakened by a fellow nun and sleepily you rise from your bed and make your way in procession to the chapel for Matins, the first of the seven canonical Hours. The only light you have with you is possibly a torch to show the community the way from the dormitory to the church.

Once you enter into the chapel in silence and begin to pray, the sanctity of being in the presence of God at such an hour feels intimate and sacred. This is very different from being in a church in the middle of the day when the sun is shining through the stained glass windows.

Nowadays our local Abbey, the Benedictine Abbey of St. Walburga, begins its day by waking at 4:20 with Matins at 4:50. I recently saw a pamphlet about St. Hildegard's Neubingen Abbey in Germany. They start even later, at 5:00, and have only five Hours instead of the usual seven. Although some of the earlier discipline has changed, I am sure that at 5:00 it is still plenty dark in Germany, especially in the dead of winter. The darkness is very deep here in Colorado at that hour, least until the spring equinox.

I often get up in the middle of the night when I can't sleep and enter into meditation for twenty minutes or so. It is a very different feeling than when I start my day at 7:00 or 8:00 with morning prayers. Somehow God feels so much more accessible in the darkness.

Many times whatever woke me up is troubling, and I find myself sobbing throughout the meditation. That's one of those "Help!" prayers that I spoke about earlier. Somehow my defenses are down in the middle of the night in a very different way than during daylight. But it is also a time when many insights come; perhaps the very silence makes them possible.

The Church understands darkness very well, and the liturgies of Holy Saturday and Christmas Eve begin without light except for the red, flickering sanctuary candle. There is always a feeling of expectation and excitement underneath the unfamiliarity of the deep stillness. As the liturgies begin, we see one candle being lit, then another, until little by little the entire church is flickering with the shimmer of hundreds of flames. Faces glow in the warm light, and the priest sings of the coming of the Light into our lives. It is solemn and joyous at the same time.

Different times of day invoke different emotional responses to our prayer, and that is how it should be. God comes to us wherever and whenever we ask Him to, and the only way He can meet us is in the life we are living right now. The darkness is a special time, but it is not better than the light, only different. We need different things at different times in our life, and I think we do ourselves no favors by running away from the darkness. Both are necessary to living fully. Later in this book I will talk about some of the descriptions of the path to union with God from some of the most influential spiritual writers of all time, St. Teresa of Avila and St. John of the Cross.

The path to finding the sacred in our lives is not easy, nor will it happen in an instant. No. It's the work of a lifetime, but there is nothing more important, nothing that will satisfy us more.

St. Augustine said famously, "My Lord, my heart is restless unless it rests in Thee." There will be times when we long so much for God that it becomes a real physical ache, like aching for the touch of a lover. Again, as the Psalmist says, "My soul is thirsting, my body pines, for You my heart is longing. Your love is better than life itself. You are the God who upholds me. You are the God whom I seek." (Ps. 63)

As we begin to make our way into the Prayer of Quiet, or Centering Prayer, or meditation, or whatever form of being with the Holy One suits us best at a particular moment, we begin to get a sense of what this whole path of life is about.

It is about finding our center, our Home.

CHAPTER 8

Standing in Fear

You might think that a chapter about fear doesn't have much to do with the spiritual life. Trust me, it does. A lot. Because when we are afraid, we can't give of ourselves and become who we really are, or I should say, Who We Really Are, i.e., children of God.

A few weeks ago one of our parish priests gave a homily about St. Paul's second letter to the Corinthians, in which Paul speaks about having "a thorn in his side." Apparently the good people of Corinth thought that Paul had abandoned them, or at least he hadn't come to see them often enough. Besides, they thought he was a terrible speaker! All of this caused Paul anguish, but he endured it for the love of Christ.

So that homily got me to thinking about what has been a thorn in the side of my life. What is the one thing that has caused me the most grief throughout the years?

It wasn't an easy question to answer, but finally I realized that the thing that has held me back the most often is fear. Just plain fear. Of everything.

Of having cold hands in folk dancing class when I was little.

Of a puppet play I saw in third grade about Ali Baba and the Forty Thieves. That one gave me nightmares for months afterwards.

I was sure those thieves were going to come right up the stairs to my room and slaughter me in my bed.

Of course, I never told anyone about my fears. What would have been the point? In my family, where emotions were suspect, I probably would have been told not to worry about it and to just go back to sleep. That was the problem! I wasn't asleep; I was WORRYING ABOUT BEING MURDERED IN MY BED!

So I sucked it up.

Maybe some of you have had similar experiences. Not so much fun, is it? After all, if I exposed my fears, what would other people think? Was I good enough, smart enough, pretty enough? Was I *enough* enough?

Do any of these normal fears ring a bell with you?

How about facing minor surgery when I was twelve? I distinctly remember riding in the front seat between my parents on the way to the hospital and being absolutely terrified—and not saying a word. Nope, gotta keep that stiff old upper lip and pretend that everything is okay. I can do this by myself, right? Yeah, sure.

This feeling of being scared of everything carried over into pretty much everything I did. I can vividly remember learning to folk dance in third or fourth grade at school. I was terrified to hold hands with other kids in the circle, because my hands were always icy cold, whereas theirs were warm, even sweaty. I was so afraid of being judged for my cold hands. So even though folk dancing was so much fun, and even became a passion for me later in life, the act of holding another person's warm hand was torture to me.

Regardless of my fear of being judged for having cold hands, by the time I reached third grade I was functioning at a high level in school, and those who knew me often commented on my poise and grace under pressure. I took drama lessons from a local woman who had me learn "readings" that were basically about characters placed in some scenario which I had memorized and performed for audiences.

One of these readings had me wearing a series of costumes, including hats and scarves, and in one instance, a long flowing skirt. I was performing this routine in a talent show, and somehow I got the skirt on wrong side out. My mom was seated in the audience close to the front, and she told me later that she could hear me say under my breath, "Oh, well. It doesn't matter. Just keep going."

And I did.

That's what I always did, I just kept going, no matter what.

But of course, there is a price to pay for such pride. Eventually, it takes a toll on your body.

So I was sick a lot as a kid. I was hiding so much and was so good at pretending that everything was okay, that I didn't even know myself that there was another way to be. Perhaps no one did, not in those days. This was all before the self-realization movement that really didn't get started until the 1980s, so who knew this stuff in 1954?

Now, we know about stress and the effect chronic stress has on the body. But then, well, if you got sick, it must be because there was a bug going around. That's just the way life was, and no one questioned it or even thought about whether or not there might be a better way to live.

I even remember consciously cultivating a feeling of being nervous as a good thing.

I was in high school by then, and still active in drama. One year, our class put on *The Diary of Anne Frank,* the inspiring story of the Dutch Jewish family who hid out in an attic above a warehouse in Amsterdam during World War II for two years before being discovered and sent to a concentration camp. The whole family perished there with the exception of Otto Frank, Anne's father. After the war was over, Otto discovered Anne's diary, which is a remarkable document about what their life was like, and how in spite of everything, Anne never lost her faith that people were basically good, even with all her evidence to the contrary.

I played the part of Edith Frank, Anne's mother, who kept the family going and never lost sight of what it meant to be Jewish. I identified so strongly with her that I imagined what she must have been feeling as they hunkered down in their attic, eight people crowded into a couple of rooms, trying to be quiet so that they would not be found.

She must have been terrified a lot of the time, each time they heard noises down below their hiding place, or they heard the war planes droning overhead. Edith was responsible for seeing that everyone was fed as well as she could, with limited resources. It could not have been easy for her.

So I cultivated feeling nervous all the time to help me get into character. I thought that was a good thing. It made me interesting, like a real actress.

But here's the rub. I forgot to let go of the nerves once the play was over. That was definitely not a good thing.

By the time I was into my mid-twenties and starting graduate school at the University of Colorado at Boulder, I was a nervous wreck. I lived on cigarettes and black coffee and lost twenty pounds. Grad school is not fun under the best of circumstances. There are orals to prepare for, which you must pass in order to graduate.

Some of the courses I loved, such as singing in madrigals, and my methods classes. I enjoyed the creativity of jazz arranging for choirs, or writing original choral works. But classes in higher education, a course that had a number of people who had been teaching at the college level for years, were way above my comfort level. So I worried a lot about whether I would ever get my Master's or not.

Now maybe you're thinking, but I've never experienced the kind of fear this author is talking about. What does this all have to do with me? Or the silence?

To which I say, well, good for you! I am very glad you didn't have to endure this unending sense of just struggling to keep up with the world and everyone else in it.

I have since learned that there is a specific personality type that worries all the time. That fit me to a T.

These people worry all the time, about everything, because they want most of all to feel secure. But most of the time they don't, so they keep thinking that if they just worry enough about everything, maybe they'll be able to keep the bad stuff from occurring. Like that's ever going to happen.

Suffice it to say, living that way is a very unpleasant way to live, because you always feel like you're not safe in your very self. So there is a lot of posturing going on to keep the chaos that you feel at bay.

That's the insidious nature of fear. It keeps us from being all that we were born to be. That's the devilish little voice of the ego saying, "Who do you think you are? You are nothing much, only a little girl from Kansas. How can you possibly know anything? You didn't graduate from Yale or Harvard, you don't have a Ph.D. in counseling, you're not a physician or a priest. How can you know enough to help someone else?"

What the ego neglects to tell us is that we have our life experience to guide us. All the classes we have ever taken, whether or not they led to an advanced degree, have contributed to our store of life knowledge. In our marriage, in our dealings with other people, all the common sense that we got from our parents and teachers along the way—all these things contribute to the person we are today.

Now, of course, I can just hear some of you saying, "But isn't fear sometimes a good thing? Doesn't it help to keep us safe from danger?"

And the answer is, yes, sure.

If you're walking down a very dark street late at night and you think you're being followed, you're right to be careful and to take precautions to get to a well-lighted place as fast as you can. If you are driving on an icy road in the winter, you are right to take it slowly and carefully so that you don't slide off into a ditch, or worse, end up having an accident. If your gut says that this or that person isn't someone you should be alone with, trust that feeling. It is helping you to put boundaries around yourself for your own protection.

In short, you should always trust your own instincts, because they are the built-in warning system that God has given us to keep us safe. It is when we don't pay attention to such warnings that we get ourselves into trouble.

Are we perfect? Of course not. But for most of the things that come up in our life, we have the smarts and the courage to get through the problem and on to the next step. Usually there are resources to help us along the way, if we just know where to look.

I've talked before about my fall, when I was totally helpless and couldn't do anything for myself. But what I didn't say is that there was always—*always*—someone there who could show me what the next step should be.

For example, when I was still in the hospital, the doctor suggested two rehab facilities for me to go to when I left. I didn't know anything about either of the two places he recommended, so I chose the one that was closer to our house so that my husband wouldn't have to drive so far. It turned out to be the perfect place that I needed to be in order to heal. (There's that idea of standing in trust again!)

When I was ready to leave rehab, there was a social worker at the facility who suggested that I have home health care for the next two months, and it was her job to take care of who those people should be. Once again, I was paired up with just the right people who could help me get to the next step.

Then when I was finished with the home health team, the physical therapist and the occupational therapist suggested a place I should go to for further treatment, and they even recommended which therapists would suit me best.

Whatever the next step was, there was always someone there to help me along the way. What a blessing that was! What could have been a horrendous experience turned out to be one of the best times of my life. Now, I am not saying that I want to repeat my stay in a rehabilitation facility, but the situation could have been so much worse. I was very lucky to have had caring and talented people to help me to get through it.

In fact, I don't remember feeling any fear at all. I didn't worry about what was to come next; I just knew I would be taken care of. It was like being inside a perfect, protected bubble. I just trusted that the process would happen as it was supposed to, and it did.

Isn't that a better way to deal with problems than the endless worrying loop our minds get into whenever we are fearful and afraid? In my mind, I hear Julian of Norwich saying, "All will be well, and all will be well, and all manner of things will be well."

Of course, Julian did *not* say that everything is going well right now, only that things will *be* well in the end. Julian knew whereof she spoke, for she lived in wartime as well as during the Black Plague in Europe, so things were not always "well," even for her.

But for me, they were. Everything that needed to happen, did, and exactly at the right time.

In fact, I would add to Julian's sunny outlook that things usually happen when they are supposed to and as a way to help us solve whatever life problem we are working on at the time.

I just wish I could have more faith that things always WILL be well, every time something happens that I don't like, instead of taking the default position of fear.

One of the easiest ways to help overcome fear is to be grateful. A gratitude journal is a wonderful way to list the things every day that we are thankful for. There are so many good things that you can soon fill up a whole book with the things you love in your life. I have kept such a journal for most of my life, and sometimes it is good to go back and re-read what I was thankful for several years ago. I realize that very often I appreciate many of the same things today.

If you are having a hard time thinking of what some of those things might be, here are some examples:

- I can see to type this sentence.
- I have a wonderful husband who is the light of my life.
- I have good friends who support me.
- My hands and fingers work, so that I can cut up vegetables and fruit for meals.
- We have warm water for our showers each morning without our having to even think about it.
- I can walk and talk, no small blessing.
- I can hear all the beautiful sounds outside: The birds singing in the morning, the coyotes in the natural area at night, yipping away, and the owls hooting at night.
- I can play with and pet my cat.
- I can enjoy watching TV.
- There is electricity to heat and cool my house so that I can stay comfortable.

Well. You get the idea. I'm sure you can think of many other good things you have in your life.

When we are thankful, our vibration or energy is actually faster and at a higher rate, unlike with fear or hatred, which are constrictive emotions that bring us down vibrationally. We can tell when our vibration is high by becoming aware of our emotions. They are the surest way to tell whether we are fully alive or not.

If we spend our time hating things, people, and the world in general, we need to pay attention to the way that hatred makes us feel. Do we feel loving and joyful? Our bodies register the two emotions very differently. In fact, our bodies are the truest barometer we have in judging whether or not our vibration is high.

Fear is one of those constrictive emotions that makes us feel tight, or cold, or as if someone has hit us in the middle of our backs. We may feel paralyzed, as if we can't move. Our hands may feel clammy or sweaty.

As we learn more about how the body reflects our thoughts, we learn that we don't have to feel bad all the time. There are things we can do to improve how we feel.

I remember it came as quite a surprise to me that we actually can choose how we feel. I had never heard that thought before, and it took a while for me to really understand the truth of it. Not only that, but I can give myself permission to feel good if I want to! Really? I don't need to ask someone else how to feel in a given situation? I can feel however I want to and not feel guilty about it? What a revelation!

If that's true, then I choose to feel good as much as I can. Why would I want to get mired down in fear or anger when I can choose joy or happiness?

Joy is another one of the expansive emotions, as are love, enthusiasm, and being kind to others. All these things make us feel better, and it's hard to be fearful when we're having fun. Try it. You'll soon see the difference.

Being out in nature is another good way to improve our mood and get ourselves out of feeling fearful. Unless of course we run into a rattlesnake while we're hiking, but how often does that really happen? I've been hiking for years, and I only saw a rattlesnake once. And it was dead. So apart from a momentary startle response, my good humor quickly returned.

Enjoying a sunny day in the mountains, or skiing, or walking in the woods in the fall when the colors are at their most beautiful is much better than staying at home growling at how awful the state of the world is.

It's my choice.

I realize I've gotten away from fear as a specifically negative emotion, but that has been on purpose, since most of the constrictive emotions make us feel bad in one way or another. Wouldn't you rather feel wonderful and alive? I know I would.

As I wrote previously, I was very surprised to learn that we can choose how we want to feel. I had never heard that before, since I came from a time and a culture in which people just took it for granted that if they experienced Scenario A, then they would automatically feel Emotion A to go along with it. But what if instead, we chose to feel Emotion B? Or even X?

"Huh," I thought. "You mean people can actually do that?" I had to ponder on that one for a bit to see if it felt right to me.

Once the thought had settled in for a while, it became clear that if it were true, then no one else had the right to make me feel guilty if I didn't feel exactly the way they thought I should feel. I would be able to choose how to experience any emotion the way it felt right to me at the time.

I remember the day of my father's funeral. It was lovely and sunny outside, and the atmosphere in my mom's house was stifling from the fifty or so people inside, all of whom were mourning and weeping. I had to get out of there, so I went for a short walk all by myself. The day was so glorious that I soon began to feel wonderful and free, while at the same time I was sad that my dad wasn't there to see it with me. All too soon, though, I began to remember that the people in the house were grieving, and I began to feel guilty for my good mood at such a melancholy time.

Today I would allow myself to feel whatever emotion arose in that moment, without castigating myself for my supposed selfishness. It is not selfish to honor our own being. It is being true to who we are. Life is too short to worry about what others think about us, if indeed they are thinking about us at all.

I may sometimes feel sad, but if I do, then I know it is my choice to do so. Whatever I choose to feel is okay. I don't have to stand in fear unless I want to. It is my choice.

CHAPTER 9

Standing on Holy Ground

Standing still is about how and why we need to get still from time to time in order to find our inner self. Sometimes we need help, not only to put ourselves in a proper frame of mind but also in a particular place that helps us to foster the quiet within. Since this chapter is about standing on holy ground, I want to spend some time talking about what exactly that term means.

Seeking out places whose energy uplifts us is a great way to deepen our faith and bring us closer to God.

We may want to visit a special place of worship because of its beauty or special significance, such as a particular church here in town where I often go just to sit and absorb the energy there. It feels like such a holy place, sitting as it does on a high hill overlooking the city to the west. The artwork is nice but not extraordinary, but there is a lovely view of the high Colorado peaks beyond the windows behind the altar. Being inside, but being able to see the outdoors, is refreshing to my soul.

From ancient times until the present, those who constructed temples, whether of Christianity or earlier religions, understood that the building itself was an important part of helping people to comprehend the Divine. In the 2016 book called *The Most Influential Figures of Ancient History*, a collaboration between *TIME* and *National Geographic*, there are some wonderful photos that illustrate that early architects grasped this concept very well. Abu Simbel, the monumental temple of Ramses II of Egypt has seated figures that are sixty feet high, and the whole edifice is carved into a stone cliff. The visitor cannot help but feel a sense of awe when looking at this magnificent structure. The Ajanta Caves chiseled by early Buddhists likewise fill the onlooker with spaciousness and wonder. Even in Athens the Parthenon of the Greeks must have been a marvel to behold in its heyday. It's still pretty spectacular, even as a ruin today.

In the mid-1970s we lived in France while my husband pursued a post-doctoral year in Grenoble, which is in the southeast in the French Alps. Because it is such an ancient city it has many old, beautiful churches, some dating from the tenth century.

The medieval churches all over Europe, but especially in France and England, were built when most of the population was illiterate, except for the priests, so the faithful learned about God by being in the sacred space where Mass was held. The high, soaring arches of Gothic churches still fill us with a sense of awe at the majesty and spaciousness of the Eternal One, and the rose windows, placed high above and behind the altar, hint at the beauty of God. Sometimes these windows are also placed at the other end of the center aisle, so that people can see them on their way out of the church.

A rose is also the symbol of love in the language of flowers, although the rose is not the only symbol that can appear in a rose window. I have seen these windows with stained glass figures of a dove, for example, which represents the Holy Spirit, or some other religious symbol. Jesus is often depicted as the Good Shepherd or the Lamb of God, and He frequently is holding a small lamb in His arms. There may also be stained glass representations of the Eucharist, such as sheaves of wheat and bunches of grapes, or the plate on which the finished bread rests along with a chalice for the wine.

I think it's unlikely the architects of that age were aware of the power of the mandala, or the circular sacred art that brings the viewer into a meditative state, but it's possible they had heard of the ancient Sanskrit word that means circle, or wheel. After all, the 12th century mystic Hildegard of Bingen designed many mandalas to represent the visions that she received all her life, starting when she was a very young child. She used the mandala to represent the world and its relationship to the Creator, or He whom she referred to as The One. She was most decidedly not a Hindu, and she probably never heard the word *mandala,* but considering that the circle is one of the most easily and widely understood forms in the universe, it's not so surprising that she used it to design her visionary artwork.

I believe that a rose window is basically a sacred Christian mandala. It is often but not always symmetric in design, which is a characteristic of mandalas, and it may have four, six, eight, or twelve divisions, each using the same colors and designs. If it is a picture of Jesus, Mary, or some other person or angel, the window will obviously not be divided into sections, unless there is a small image that does repeat in the design, such as a vine with leaves, grapes, or sheaves of wheat, all of which represent the Eucharist.

Very often traditional Sanskrit mandalas place the circle within a square which has four gates or doors at the cardinal points. The circle represents wholeness or the Universe, as well as reminding us of our relationship to the eternal God and wholeness, while the four gates are ways into the sacred space.

In that sense, then, the mandala is most certainly a sacred space, because gazing at one or meditating upon it allows the viewer to fall into that place that is both within us and beyond us, both of the present moment and in the eternal Now.

The labyrinth is another sacred symbol of our journey to God, our center. (This is not the same thing as the labyrinth in the Greek story of Theseus and the Minotaur, which would more properly be called a maze.) The labyrinth used as a prayer device since about the middle of the 14th century is a mandala that is on the ground, if it is outside, or painted or tiled into the floor if it is inside a building. It is designed to be used as a meditative walking prayer, because the walker begins on the outside and slowly works his or her way to the center of the design.

There is only one path in and out of the circle that leads to God, and it takes the pray-er first close to, but not quite inside the center, and then back out. The design repeats four times, marking the four directions as well as forming the arms of a cross. Only the final leg of the journey actually leads to the center. It can be a very profound experience. Walking slowly thus becomes another form of meditation; instead of standing or sitting still in the lotus position or with one's feet solidly on the ground; the very purposefulness of the walking meditation can produce deep relaxation and peace.

Mandalas certainly can be very beautiful, but their main purpose is to encourage viewers simply to gaze into their depths and see what is opened up inside of themselves. Different designs can elicit very different and sometimes powerful feelings, which can be of great benefit to the one doing the gazing. It can be a kind of praying without words, instead using pictures or images.

Today mandala coloring books are very popular with adults who might like to have a way to center themselves in a physical prayer. They can be found at many bookstores, and the designs, which are all different, elicit different feelings and emotions in the one who colors them. They can be a way for us to explore our creativity in using crayons, markers, or colored pencils to design the color scheme for our mandala. It may also inspire us to draw our own mandalas.

What things, for example, do lotus petals mean to you? How about twining vines, or crosses, or fruits of various kinds? Your emotions and insights may be different from those of someone else, and that is okay. We don't all need to have the same experiences, but some themes are more or less universal. The wheel can represent the wheel of life, for example, and lotus blossoms, also sometimes called water lilies, often conjure up the opening of the self to God. The longer we allow ourselves to just look at a mandala without expectations or judgments of any kind, the more beneficial it will be.

Certainly the men who put rose windows into cathedrals understood this concept, even if they had never heard the word *mandala*. They most certainly had heard of the love God has for His people. Those who designed and built these monuments to God knew what they were about. They understood that people can learn things subliminally, without knowing they are learning anything at all, and they used space to create places where worshippers could wonder about who God is, and their relationship to Him.

I always feel the holiness of such expansive buildings; they feel like holy ground.

The stained-glass windows often tell the Biblical stories, such as Noah and the Flood, or the Creation of the World; they may depict Jesus as the Good Shepherd, or the time He turned water into wine at the wedding at Cana of Galilee. Sometimes there also may be pictures of some of the saints, especially the patron saint of the particular church. St. Peter and St. Paul are popular choices, as is Mary, the mother of Jesus. Other times there may be symbols represented, such as sheaves of wheat or fat purple grapes that are used in the Eucharist, stand-ins for Jesus's Body and Blood.

Many of the ancient churches and cathedrals also contain the tombs of saints or famous people, so one also feels the weight of history just by being in these spaces. Sometimes these tombs are in the church proper; at other times, there is a crypt below the main church where Mass might be celebrated on the saint's feast day or another sacred occasion.

If you are ever in Paris and have the chance to visit Notre Dame, you will know what I mean about the weight of history. This church, after all, saw the crowning of Napoleon and Charlemagne, as well as the kings and queens of France, so it is far more than just a sacred space. It is a repository for history. It has beautiful rose windows, as well.

There are many variations on the way the designer and builders of different churches thought about God and the relationship of the people who worshipped there. For instance, one time when we were in Ecuador we went to Mass in a medium-sized church that had a rather distinct personality. The first thing we noticed was the abundance of mirrors set all around the interior space and facing out to the outside. I asked someone what the purpose of those mirrors was, and she said that when the early Spaniards brought Christianity to South America, many of the native tribes were afraid to enter a church, never having seen one before. So the missionaries explained that the mirrors were to repel evil spirits. The Indians were comforted by this explanation, figuring that a church couldn't be all bad if the plan was not to let any evil come inside.

Another curious aspect of this particular church was that all the statues of Jesus, Mary, and Joseph plus many others were wearing real clothing, such as one female saint who sported a pink tutu and a glittering tiara and an elderly gentleman in a comfortable bathrobe and house slippers. The same woman I had talked to before said that the parish had a whole committee of women whose job it was to make sure that the statues were decked out in their finery, which changed with the seasons. For Christmas they would wear something more festive than during Lent, for example, and when it was cold outside, they wore coats and hats.

Still another thing that happened brought home to me just how comfortable the people were with "their" parish. During the most sacred part of the Mass, a big black Lab trotted up the center aisle. Nobody blinked an eye. He made his way into the sanctuary, where he lay down on the floor and took a nap, quite at home. Perhaps he belonged to the priest, but he had obviously done this many times, and no one thought anything about it. He was as welcome to be at Mass as anyone else.

Contrast that homey feeling with a very small Swiss parish that seemed rather staid and unremarkable. It was certainly serviceable for having Mass, but it was just an average church in a workingclass neighborhood. The holiness in that space came from the people who worshiped there, not from gorgeous art or spectacular stained glass windows.

And then there is the majesty that is apparent at St. Peter's in Rome. Obviously no expense was spared here; the whole place is so splendid that the visitor can hardly take it all in. We were there for the New Year's Day Mass in 1976, which closed a Holy Year, so there was also the ceremony of the closing of the special doors that are only open during this special time.

Pope Paul VI was carried down the main aisle on a litter, so that everyone could see him. The Mass was a feast of song, incense, and high ritual, with the readings done in several different languages so that anyone visiting from any country would feel at home.

Another very sweet, family-feeling church was one we attended on a Native American reservation in Montana. Again, the church building was unremarkable; it was the people who made it special. When it came time for the gifts to be brought forward and presented to the priest for consecration, the celebrant simply said, "Well, Frank, why don't you take up the collection now." The tiny little parish had only about twenty people, so it didn't take long, but the whole attitude was, "This is your house, please be comfortable here." Churches are intended to represent the house of God, but they are also for the people who worship there.

In addition to seeing the great variety of churches, visiting the Holy Land, where Judaism, Christianity, and Islam all began is a wonderful place to get an understanding of how one culture influenced others. Dipping my toes into the River Jordan and seeing where, even today, baptisms take place, I was amazed at what a small stream the Jordan is. Somehow we always hear about the "mighty Jordan River" which I imagined would be a wild and rushing torrent. It's not.

It is hardly twenty yards across and seems to be quite shallow. Time and nature probably have altered the original landscape from when John the Baptist was preaching there, but the fact is that the Jordan is much smaller in reality than the way I had always pictured it. (See Matthew, Chapter 3 and Mark, Chapter 1, verses 1-11 for more on John's mission. In St. Luke's version, it is in the first part of Chapter 3, and St. John the Evangelist has the story in Chapter 1, verses 10-34.)

The area where baptisms take place has wide, shallow steps for the candidates to wait their turn to be dipped into the green water, but there are some other, smaller steps that you can go down that are not roped off as the large baptismal area is.

For some reason I was surprised that it was full of tiny minnows darting about. I tried so hard not to step on any of them! But they are quite agile, and managed to get out of my way for the most part. I think I would have remembered hitting one or more of them with my foot!

As is usual with these sacred sites, there is an air-conditioned snack bar and souvenir stand at the top of the small rise that leads down to the water, and since it is nearly always hot there, we did as thousands of others do every year and stopped in for a cold drink and something to eat. It was a relief to be out of the scorching heat, but the commercialism of the site took something away from the holy feeling of the place.

We also visited Mary's Well in Nazareth, realizing that the Blessed Mother probably came here every day to fill her water pitcher. Again, this site has the roped-off well down below, with a gaudy church built over it. You can get a small vial of the holy water if you want to take home a souvenir, and the spring at this holy site still provides drinking water for the town.

And what about being at the Sea of Galilee, where Jesus discovered Peter, Andrew, James, and John, and asked them to follow Him? (This story is also in Matthew, Chapter 4, verses 18-22; Mark, Chapter 1, verses 16-20; Luke, Chapter 5, verses 1-11; and John, Chapter 1, verses 35-50.)

When you look out over the Sea, you can easily imagine Jesus being asleep on a cushion in the rear of that sinking boat when Peter frantically came to wake Him up and ask Him to save the Apostles from drowning. (Matthew 8:23-27; Luke 8:22-25.)

In Jerusalem you can walk the Via Dolorosa, which is the street where Jesus walked carrying His cross to Calvary. And while the ancient streets are now filled with vendors selling everything you can possibly imagine, you can also visit His tomb in the Church of the Holy Sepulchre. The Passion and Death of Jesus are recounted in all of the Gospels.

I was amazed by how tiny the little marble slab was on which they laid Jesus' body after the Crucifixion. It was hard to think of a man we think of as being larger than life as being so short. And because the church that has been built over the tomb is so full of gold and silver, somehow the place didn't feel as holy to me as some of the other sites did. I personally would have preferred to see a tomb hallowed out of the bare rock, just as it would have been in Jesus' time, rather than the frankly gaudy display that some misguided architect must have thought would enhance the experience. Sometimes the holy place is enough just as it is.

One of the most memorable places for me in Jerusalem was the olive-oil-jar-shaped building that houses the Dead Sea Scrolls. These were found in 1947, and contain one of the largest pieces of actual Biblical writing extant today. It's an incomplete fragment, but it winds around the interior of the outer wall and is obviously quite large. It's amazing to realize just how old it really is.

Unfortunately the scroll is incomplete because the Egyptian farmer who found the original olive jars that held the sacred writings had no clue as to what he had found, and he burned several pages of the scroll to make the fire to cook his dinner before suddenly realizing that maybe this was something he should tell the authorities about.

As you travel from the outside world down into the bottom of the "olive oil jar," you pass an exhibit about the Essenes, the sect that John the Baptist and possibly even Jesus, belonged to for a time. One of the exhibits has olive pits, date pits, remains of cooking fires, even leather and rope sandals. I couldn't help but wonder if Jesus had worn those shoes, or had those olives and dates for dinner some long-ago night. That was one of the most moving of the places we visited.

Outside this amazing building is a large three-dimensional model of the way the Temple of the Second Period would have looked during Jesus' time. It's quite large, and you can walk all around it while looking down on it from viewing sites above it.

You can see the outer courtyard, where Peter and the rest of the crowd waited around the warming fires all during the long night of Jesus' trial, and where Peter eventually ended up denying that he even knew Jesus. The actual trial would have been in the inner courtyard, out of the sight of the common folk.

Seeing this wondrous building made the Gospels come alive for me. The story is in all four versions.

Another special place was the Upper Room, which is located in the same building where King David's tomb is on the first floor. The Upper Room itself is quite large, which surprised me, but the guide pointed out that someone had to cook the Last Supper for the Apostles and Jesus, so there might well have been two hundred people or more present, including women and children. For sure, it wouldn't have been the Apostles doing the cooking!

I had never thought about the fact that there would have been many women and children there as well as the main characters that we hear about on Holy Thursday and Pentecost, but being in the actual physical place made the Gospel accounts much more real. Just the realization that the Apostles had wives and families who also followed Jesus was eye-opening for me. It made all of the characters more like real people that you might actually know, instead of being in a story that someone wrote down. Perhaps we have all seen too many pieces of art that depict the Last Supper with only the twelve Apostles and Jesus, so we think that DaVinci's version showed the way it really was. Well, it wasn't like that at all.

For one thing, Jesus had commissioned 72 disciples to go and spread the Good News to the people, so they were probably in Jerusalem for the Passover, just as all devout Jews would have been. No doubt they were celebrating the feast with Jesus and the Twelve along with other family members and friends, real people living in Israel during the Roman occupation and doing their best to keep the Biblical commandments. They lived by the words of the Psalms and the Prophets, who were for them living examples of how to worship God. Somehow, we so often lose sight of that fact, and they become just characters in a familiar story that we have heard all of our lives, more like people in a novel rather than actual folks who ended up changing the course of history.

Standing on the holy ground of Jerusalem, Nazareth, and the Sea of Galilee changed my perspective. It deepened my respect and love for the people involved. I can never hear the Gospel stories the same way again.

One of the most interesting experiences I had was to attend a family wedding once while we were in Tel Aviv. The day before the ceremony, there was a special rite in which the groom was called to the Torah for the first time since his Bar Mitzvah. It was held in a synagogue in which the men were separated from the women by a long, opaque curtain. The men sat on the side with the Torah where all the action took place, while the women were segregated on the other side of the veil where we could neither see nor hear what was going on. Of course, most of us were soon bored and started to converse among ourselves. It was a long ceremony, more than an hour, but we had no clue as to what was actually taking place.

So then I began to think about the section in St. Paul's Letter to the Corinthians, chapter 14, verses 34-35, in which he says that women should not talk in the synagogue. Oftentimes this passage has been interpreted as meaning that women should not preach, but I wonder if maybe he simply got tired of hearing the women chattering on the other side of the curtain. Perhaps he really was saying, "Oh, for heaven's sake, you loud women! Be still and let us men pray over here! If you have questions about what we are saying, ask your husbands later in private." That puts a whole other meaning to that passage, doesn't it?

I had been back in the States for several years when I happened to come across a commentary by Joseph Tkach which says somewhat the same thing. So perhaps my interpretation isn't so far off after all.

While we're on the subject of being in the synagogue, I once had a quite different experience at a young cousin's Bar Mitzvah in Houston, Texas. This was a modern building, which looked quite a lot like any regular Christian church, with the exception of not having a cross over the altar.

As the service proceeded, I felt right at home, except for the unfamiliar music. The readings were read from the Torah in English, and naturally they were all from the Old Testament, but that is the way our Mass begins as well. So it all seemed very familiar to me with the exception of the cantor singing in Hebrew. When it ended, the rabbi, the cantor, and the Bar Mitzvah boy processed around the entire congregation, presenting the sacred scroll for veneration by all the people. It was very moving and reverent.

Now here is the part that absolutely blew me away. When the liturgy had concluded, everyone repaired to the Fellowship Hall, where the rabbi took a loaf of *challah*, the special Sabbath braided bread, blessed it, and broke it into pieces, giving each person a bite to eat. Sounds very much like our Eucharist, doesn't it? After the breaking of the bread, the rabbi blessed the wine as well, and everyone shared the cup.

I was thunderstruck with the idea that Jesus had probably been present at many of these Friday night liturgies in His lifetime. Our

Eucharist devolves directly from the Jewish tradition of breaking the bread and drinking the wine, with the addition of the words that Jesus said at the Last Supper: "This is My Body, this is My Blood. Take and eat it and drink from the cup. Do this in memory of Me." This is the way the early Christians must have experienced the Mass, because most of them were Jewish.

A Jewish friend of mine also informed me about another thing we Catholics take for granted that has its roots in early Judaism. That is the belief that Jesus died for our sins. According to this friend, the idea of someone dying for the sins of the people is part of the ceremony of Yom Kippur, or the Day of Atonement, which is described in Chapter 16 of Leviticus.

The rabbi who was leading the liturgy at the Temple in Jerusalem would take a goat kid into the Holy of Holies, that special interior place reserved only for the chief priest, and symbolically transfer the sins of the people onto the animal. The goat thus became the "scapegoat" for the people. It was then turned out into the desert, there to die of starvation, thirst, or by being eaten by prey. So when Jesus was said to have died for the sins of the people, they began to call Him the Lamb of God. They did not choose to call Him a goat, because the Gospel writers divided the people into two groups: the good people were the sheep, the ones who followed the Lord, and the goats were considered the lesser ones who did not. Even so, young goats were an acceptable sacrifice at the Temple as well.

I am always totally amazed that we Christians are never taught all these practices which started as part of regular Jewish worship and were then transformed into our Mass. I think we would be so much more captivated by our own story if we really understood what it was all about and where it came from. Such knowledge might even help us to be more respectful of other people's beliefs and practices, for what could be more sacred than a place where worship is practiced?

Holy ground can be anywhere, actually, since God created the entire world, but Israel is called the Holy Land for good reason. Three major world religions have their roots there in the land of Abraham, Isaac, and Jacob: The Jewish people, who followed Moses back to Israel from their exile in Egypt, Jesus and His followers who became the Christians, and Mohammed and the teachings of Islam. It is holy to so many.

While visiting the sacred sites of the Holy Land is wonderful, not everyone has the means or the physical stamina to make such a trip. Films about Israel can be acceptable substitutes. I saw one of them just last year at the Imax Theater at the Denver Museum of Nature and Science, and public television shows films from time to time about the area, especially during the Easter and Passover seasons.

Other pilgrimage places that may be of interest are the healing sites of Lourdes in France, and Medjugorje in Bosnia and Herzegovina, where the Virgin is said to have appeared many times. Mecca is of course the pilgrimage site devout Muslims are expected to visit at least once in their lifetime. There are many sacred places to visit in India as well. All of these locations draw huge crowds, so check before you go for tourist information. A wealth of material is available on the Web.

Holy ground can be anywhere, really. But what about places that have seen horrific acts such as wars, famines, man-made disasters of all kinds, and atrocities? Are these places still holy?

It's a fair question.

When we were in Germany one time we went on a tour that ended up at a town called Berchtesgaden. This is a little place that Hitler used as a summer town for his senior staff members and their families. It had a school for the children, a gym, and of course, many sumptuous mansions where Goebbels, Goering, and the other high-ranking officers lived. Higher up on the mountain was the Eagles' Nest, which was the command center for the Nazi regime during the hot months when they were trying to escape the Berlin heat.

There is a small village next to the now abandoned Nazi retreat where one can get souvenirs, snacks, and other services. It is still a real town.

As I was perusing the items for sale in one of the kiosks, I was struck by the number and variety of DVDs about Hitler, his life, and the Nazis. I wasn't sure if the place represented a memorial to the man and his loathsome ideas, or if the books and other information were for learning purposes only.

However, from what I understand, the German people feel so ashamed of what their nation became during the years of World War II that they want to make sure those atrocities never happen again. To that end they are dismantling as much as they can of the town, but some of the homes still belong to the descendants of the original Nazi owners and are thus off-limits to being razed. Nonetheless, the Germans seem determined to make amends to the world for what happened there.

The interesting thing in all of this was the energy that surrounded the town. Because it is high in the mountains, there are beautiful forests all around, but as we were driving up the hills, I could feel a sadness that seemed to be coming from the trees and from the very earth itself. I am sure that having soaked up all the negativity and hatred that must have been there for so many years, the place is still trying to heal itself. It felt as if it had been wounded.

I was newer to energy work then, and I didn't understand everything I was feeling, but it made a huge impression on me, so much so that I really didn't ever want to return to Germany again for any reason.

So can we say that Berchtesgaden is a holy place? So many atrocities were planned and carried out from this beautiful spot that it is hard to think of it as holy, although the land itself did nothing wrong. Wounded, for sure, and defiled, it is more like a woman who has been raped. The area has been desecrated, or de-sanctified, by the injuries done here. The insult to the place was not of Mother Earth's making, as the woman's rape was also not her fault, but both things did occur, and it will take time before it—and she—can be made whole again. I am sure that the efforts of the German people to return the town to its pre-War condition will help a lot in its healing; the woman who has been raped will more than likely need therapeutic help to reclaim her sacred self. Healing is possible and necessary in both cases.

The same thing can be said about Auschwitz and other prison camps where horrific events have taken place. They were certainly not holy spaces during World War II, but now that the war is over, and the German people have finally accepted their share of the blame for the atrocities that happened, they seem to be trying to make amends to the world.

Just as the people of Germany are investing in making their spirits whole again, I have to believe that the earth also is trying to heal itself, even though it may take many years or decades before the transformation back to holy ground is complete.

Some places become holy by virtue of the events that happen there. The area of lower Manhattan in New York is like that, especially since the fall of the Twin Towers. It has become hallowed ground precisely *because* of those nearly three thousand souls who lost their lives in the attack on September 11, 2001. The heroic efforts of the hundreds of men and women who helped to clean up the horrendous devastation that took place there assisted greatly in replacing negative energy with goodness and selfless love.

Those first responders and later the people who sifted through the piles of debris searching for the remains of those who fell from the Towers consecrated that ground with their own blood and healing energy. Many of those people have since developed cancers and other illnesses because of their high exposure to the toxins that were in the asbestos and other chemicals that were in the Towers as they fell. Naturally all of that pulverized dust had also been contaminated by the planes which slammed into the buildings that blew apart in the attack.

That ground is surely sacred, in the same way that cemeteries are holy spaces. For many of those who fell that day, it is a true burial site, for their remains still lie under the soil and will probably never be found. They will forever be buried in the rubble, and their sacrifices are now memorialized at Ground Zero, as the site is now called. Pope Francis recently visited the memorial to those who fell on 9/11. He was quoted as saying that he could still feel the grief rising from the ground, but he recognized the special spiritual quality that is also present there.

There is a feeling of desolation, almost of violation, when you visit the killing ground at Gettysburg, Pennsylvania, the site of ferocious fighting during our own Civil War. Such scenes of horror, no matter where they occur, always take time to recover, but the fact that so many people suffered and died because they belonged to the "wrong" religion, or had the "wrong" color skin, or the "wrong" belief system have served to sanctify these places as well. I am sure that someday visitors to these battlegrounds will come to recognize them as hallowed ground, much as President Lincoln did when he wrote the Gettysburg Address after the Civil War was over.

Surprisingly enough, the beaches at Normandy feel much more normal than either Berchtesgaden or Ground Zero. I think it may be because the French people have worked hard to make sure that in addition to the fact that so many died there, they also understood that the American and Belgian soldiers were trying to save Western Europe by their sacrifice.

The French have also made sure that the land is available for people trying to live a regular life today, so the beaches are open to camping and picnics, swimming and walking along the sands. I am sure that the Normandy beaches are receiving a lot of energy that is based in joy, children's laughter, and love, and that they are healing faster than some other places as a result.

Wars are one thing you say, but what about natural disasters? What of the tsunamis in Japan and Malaysia, or the earthquakes or hurricanes that regularly seem to hit Nepal or Haiti? It's almost always the poorest of the poor who suffer the most, because they have no political power to demand that their homes be built to withstand these naturally occurring events, but surely their lands are no less blessed by God than those of us who are fortunate to have adequate housing and clean water.

I think that those who live close to the earth recognize its holiness, for it gives them food to eat, water to drink, and air to breathe. They understand that the earth is our mother and needs to be taken care of, as one would take care of anything else that is beloved. The earth is certainly holy to them.

St. Hildegard of Bingen, one of my favorite saints, and one of the most prolific writers who ever lived, had a lot to say about the environment. She lived in Germany from 1098 to 1179 when she died at 81, which for the times was an old lady. During her long lifetime, she wrote many books, some of which described what it means to be holy. She was a big fan of environmentalism, even though it wasn't called that in her day. She respected the earth and everything which lived on it, and that for her was equated with what she called *viriditas*, or greening.

Living as she did along the Rhine River in Germany, she would have been keenly aware of the lush green growth in that area, and she likened that green beauty to the soul's connection to God. She noticed that all the plants that grow become green. If they wither, they will die. If they are cut off from the vine that gives them life, they also will die, so greening, or *viriditas*, is extremely important if we are at all interested in leading a spiritual life. Dryness for Hildegard was the worst possible sin, for it meant that we are not connected to God who is the Divine Vine.

Hildegard certainly understood the concept of holy ground; even though she never wrote about such a thing, it was evident in the care she took to situate the two convents she built, Rupertsberg and later Eibingen, on the most beautiful land she could find. Both monasteries were built on mountaintops overlooking the Rhine, because she understood that natural beauty helps the soul to connect with God. In fact, the very name of Rupertsberg means "Rupert's Mountain." Rupert was a local saint who was much beloved in Hildegard's time.

Meditation usually is a large part of living the monastic life, so we would expect that a monastery or convent is a holy place. Is the space where we meditate holy ground?. Of course it is. If we dedicate ourselves to holiness whenever we meditate, the space where we pray becomes holy by our actions there.

We are the ones who have to make a place holy. By our actions and our thoughts, and our view of who is worthy or not, of being "acceptable" or not, we show ourselves to be in alignment or not with God. One who continually labels everyone who disagrees with him as being a "loser" is not aligned with God. One who bullies others on the internet to the point of causing them to commit suicide is not aligned with God. As St. John the Evangelist puts it in his Gospel: "God is love, and all who live in love, live in God." (I John 4:16)

Those who rape, or murder, or torture other human beings or animals, or who desecrate the planet by fouling its waters, its oceans, its air, or its earth are the driest of the dry, to put it in Hildegard's terms. Her teaching about *viriditas,* or green-ness, is one that resonates with those of us for whom caring about the earth is a way of being spiritual and connected to the One who made all things. The native peoples have also always respected the earth and taken care of it, for they understood that if we don't take care of it, ultimately it—and we—will die. We are all connected, and our intention here is key: If we believe in the sacredness of our environment, then we will take care of it. It is up to each of us to make the ground where we live, work, and play a holy place.

It starts with the home. Is our home a refuge for our family at the end of a long day of work or school? What things feed our souls at home?

Perhaps you love plants and flowers, and your home always has green and growing things. Does that help to nourish you by furnishing beauty for you to enjoy? How about the music you listen to? Do the songs speak respectfully about women, children, and lovers? These things have a way of getting into our subconscious, whether we know it or not, and songs that glorify rape or drugs do not really sustain a healthy life.

The same thing can be said for the TV shows we are addicted to. Are they fun and relaxing, or are they "reality" shows that in reality are heavily scripted to show the worst side of human behavior? Shows that focus on backstabbing, vampires, scheming on ways to get revenge on someone who has ostensibly harmed us, or constantly use foul language don't really do very much to uplift us.

We want our living space to reflect who we are, but our homes don't have to be expensively decorated with the latest and greatest appliances or artwork to be attractive and welcoming. What makes a house a home is the welcoming attitude of those who live there and love each other. When we respect those with whom we share living space, it doesn't matter what the place looks like. It has an energy that says to everyone who enters, "This is a happy place to be, and I would like to spend time with the people who live here." That matters so much more than whether or not we have the most up-to-date furnishings or color scheme.

Some places, of course, are inherently holy as we discussed before, like monasteries and convents, and other places where people gather to live in community for the purpose of becoming closer to God. Yet even here, intention is the key.

There is a Benedictine abbey in the mountains west of my town, the Abbey of St. Walburga, that exemplifies all that is good and holy. St. Walburga, according to the small book about her that I found in their gift shop, was an English noblewoman from a good Catholic family. She and her parents and two brothers emigrated to Germany to help St. Boniface, who was some sort of cousin, in his efforts to spread the faith. They must have been successful, for all of St. Walburga's family—she, her parents and two brothers—are canonized saints. St. Walburga was quite a healer in her day, and even now, a statue of her in Germany "weeps" with what is called St. Walburga's Oil, said to be beneficial in helping to cure many ailments.

The Abbey that bears her name is situated up near the Wyoming border in a beautiful area of the rocky foothills. It has such an air of peace and tranquility that the visitor knows right away that it is a holy place.

And that is one of the ways we can tell if a place is holy or not. How does it make us feel to be there? Holiness has a feeling about it, an energy that emanates from it that lets us know, sometimes very subtly, sometimes more forcefully: This is sacred ground. Treat it with respect.

But there is another kind of holy ground that is exceptional and rare, simply by being extraordinarily beautiful and special. These places are often national parks, because governments recognize that something this unique deserves to be preserved for all people for all time.

Think about the Grand Canyon, for example. If one spends any time there at all—and to really experience it, you must spend at least a full day, if not a full week—you will find yourself at a loss for words to describe the enormity of it.

People who venture away from the touristy area near El Tovar Hotel often are totally silent, gazing in wonder at the huge chasm that time and water have created. It is easy to spend the whole day just marveling at the play of light and shadows across the rocky formations and watching for the California condors which soar and glide above the Canyon's depths. God seems to be very much present in such a place.

One time my husband and I drove the two hundred miles from the South Rim around to the north side of the Canyon. Whereas the

South Rim is very desert-like, the North Rim is nearly a mile higher in elevation, and the vegetation is very different. The North Rim sees many fewer visitors, since it is so much harder to get to and it is not open all year round as the South Rim is, but its very isolation makes it far more special. We hiked along the Rim Trail and were by ourselves for most of the time. It was easy to find a flat rock to sit on and meditate, and the scent of the pines and the crisp breeze were very refreshing. It would be hard to find a cathedral that is more beautiful or more sacred than the North Rim of the Canyon.

The light is different here, too. The sun hits the rocks at a different angle, and things that we thought we recognized on the other side of the canyon suddenly took on a whole different character.

Both Rims had an abundance of golden mantled ground squirrels begging for crumbs from our lunch, and both had canyon wrens singing from the high cliffs, but the experience was different, depending on which Rim we were on.

Another wonderful way to see the Canyon is to hike down into it. It is probably better to do this hike in the spring or fall, or even the winter, because the summer temperatures can easily rise above 100 degrees. We once hiked partway down into the Canyon, and we didn't take nearly enough water with us. We were forced to turn around at Indian Gardens to be sure we didn't suffer from heat stroke just trying to get out. When we had the "desert experience" that day, we got a sense of what it must have been like for Jesus to spend forty days alone in the uninhabited regions that He knew so well.

We also spent a day in the Israeli desert one time near the Dead Sea, and it's no wonder that Moses and his people were lost there for forty years. It all looks alike. How would we tell someone where to go, "Turn right at the white rocks?" Guess what—it's *all* white rocks!

I know the Israelis say that the reason Moses stayed so long in the desert was to let the older generation die off so that the younger people would be the ones who reached the Promised Land, but our experience made the" getting lost" story seem very plausible, too.

A totally different experience is to be found at Carlsbad Caverns in southern New Mexico. As I was starting down the path into the depths of the caverns, I kept turning around to look up at the entrance which was getting smaller and smaller the further down we descended. At first, I was a little leery of leaving the daylight behind, but as we got deeper into the cave, the wonders we were seeing began to grab my whole attention.

The stalactites and stalagmites are subtly illuminated to highlight the most beautiful features, and the variety of colors and textures soon had me entranced.

When we got all the way to the bottom, most of the tourists had had enough, it seemed, and had already taken the elevator back up to the top, so we pretty much had the whole place to ourselves, which was amazing.

The sound of the silence was deafening. Yes, there is an actual sound of silence. We could almost feel the earth pulsing, which made it feel as if it were breathing. The silence went *kawhang, kawhang, kawhang* against our eardrums. It was eerie.

The stillness was so vast that we couldn't *not* meditate. So we sat on some rocks and did just that. It was stupefyingly, staggeringly awesome, in the real sense of the word, and words are not adequate to express the feeling that we had that day. It felt as if we were inside a deep, dark womb, safe and protected and connected to the earth itself.

I have never had another experience as amazing as that was. *This* is what I often think of when I think of being with God. Just this.

Carlsbad is remarkable for another reason, as well. Bats. Thousands of bats make their homes in some of the unused, un-touristy caves that make up the whole complex. We knew we were not likely to run into a bat in the caverns, and we didn't worry about them wanting to fly into our hair. They echo-locate, and they wanted to avoid us as much as we wanted to avoid them.

But here's the amazing thing. Every night, thousands of them come out of the depths to fly off to Texas to eat mosquitos. And we watched them do it. There is an amphitheater just outside the entrance to the Caverns, situated on a hillside where we could see both the entrance and the sky above.

We smelled the bats long before we saw them, a sweet-ish aroma that alerted us to their presence. Then came the rush of thousands of wings beating together, a totally magnificent sound. All at once—there they were! A huge, black clot of bats, all winging their way to Texas for their night of munching on mosquitos.

The whole process took probably ten minutes, at most, yet it was one of those heart-stoppingly sublime and glorious experiences that took us out of ourselves, and we were aware of how majestic and grand nature really is. If people are at all aware of God, they will certainly see and feel His presence in such an event.

Obviously, we are not the first people on earth to think of some special places as being particularly holy. One such group is the Hopi Indian tribe, who live in Arizona within the Navajo reservation. For the Hopi people, the San Francisco Peaks north of Flagstaff are their holy place. They believe that the *kachinas*, or their sacred beings, make their home on the high places.

We are not so different from the indigenous tribes in that respect. The sacredness of such holy ground often gives people a sense of connection to something far bigger than we are. Even as far back as Moses' time, people understood that God, or Yahweh, was on the mountaintop. That is why Moses went up on the mountain to receive the Ten Commandments.

Now we know that God is not just on the mountain, but that the One Who is the All can be everywhere and nowhere at the same time. However, the mountains still speak to us of the wonder and high stature of God. The mountains often do feel like secure places for us, because they seem to be unchanging, as God is. They are solid and strong, and they provide barriers from our enemies, or at least in Old Testament times they did. They seem to be eternal.

Nature is also awesome in a different way, for there are green and growing things that inspire the same kind of wonder and awe. Think of the giant redwoods and sequoias that have been around since Jesus' time, and it's almost hard to imagine the time span for these wondrous trees. We begin to get a sense of the wonder and power of God, who created this beauty for us to enjoy. Any gorgeous scenic spot can fill our hearts with reverence for the Divine. That is why so many people seek out the solitude and splendor of nature in all her diversity.

Holy ground can be anywhere we encounter the living God and feel His presence there.

If we are sad or afraid, we may feel better just by being there and gazing on such magnificence. If we are wrestling with a thorny problem, perhaps just being in the beauty and silence of nature can help us find the solution. It's very hard to be still enough in our busy 24/7 world to find a holy place for reflection.

We all need to find such time and space to go within and be still. The quietude helps us remember who we really are.

We need to make time to stand on holy ground, whether that means a trip into nature or inside the sacred space of our own home.

Upper Room

The picture shows Cathy, the guide, and Pedro Engel in the Upper Room, which is actually a large banquet hall. This room is where the Last Supper took place. It holds about 150 people.

Western Wall of the Second Temple

The Western Wall, also sometimes called the Wailing Wall, is the only remaining part of the Second Temple which was destroyed around 70 C.E. People often come to the Wall to leave written prayers in the cracks between the stones. The large golden dome is The Dome of the Rock, which is said to mark the spot where Abraham was planning to sacrifice Isaac before God provided a ram instead. The Rock is sacred to Islam as well, as it is thought to be where Mohammed ascended into heaven.

Jordan River

This is the baptismal area where many people come to receive the sacrament of Baptism at the same spot where John is said to have baptized Jesus. John called the people to repent of their sins, and the water of the Jordan was believed to cleanse away any imperfections so that they could then turn their lives around.

There is another area, not roped off as this spot is, where we dipped our feet into the cool water. There were so many minnows here!

The river is very narrow at this point, not at all the "great river" of the Scriptures.

Israel Museum

The Israel Museum in Jerusalem contains a remnant of the Dead Sea Scrolls, which wraps around the interior of the lower level of an olive-oil-jar shaped building. This photo is from outside the actual museum and is a huge replica of the way Jerusalem would have looked in Jesus' time. At the top is the Holy of Holies, which could only be entered by the High Priest during certain ceremonies. The inner courtyard was where Jesus' actual trial took place, and the outer courtyard, seen here on the right, would have been where Peter and the rest of the crowd would have been waiting for the result.

Israeli Desert

This photo shows the Israeli desert near the Dead Sea. It makes the story of Moses and his group being lost for 40 years seem very plausible. Everything looks the same, and very little grows here on the ever-present white rocks. No wonder they needed manna to eat.

Church of the Holy Sepulchre, Jerusalem

The entrance showing the front of the church. There is now a market, or *souk,* along the original Way of the Cross. It sells everything from spices to clothing and jewelry and is a popular tourist destination. It is quite near to the original Temple, but it's all uphill, so it would have been very difficult for Jesus to carry His cross.

CHAPTER 10

Standing in Holiness

While I understand that many people meditate in order to find relaxation or to reduce stress, that will not be the focus of this particular chapter. Since this book is primarily my own spiritual memoir, I am writing mostly about my own journey. Thus, while those other goals are certainly useful and appropriate functions of standing still, my intention is to approach stillness as a way that leads the practitioner to become closer to the God who is the Source of our being, the One who is the All. In this type of meditation, the goal is to make the time one spends sitting in stillness into an opportunity to "be present to the Presence."

There is a difference between trying to become whole and trying to become holy, although the two words both derive from the same Old English word (before 900 C.E.) *hal*, or *haleg* for holy, which meant both whole and wholeness. In my view, when one is attempting to become a whole person, that undertaking also includes the interior aspect that I am calling holiness. In fact, many spiritual writers would agree that for a person to become a fully whole being, then that would by definition include striving to attain holiness. One is not one without the other.

The definitions I am using in all of this discussion can be found in the Random House Webster's *College Dictionary*, copyrighted in 1999, with a second edition revised and updated in 2000.

There is another distinction that I feel is important here, and that is the difference between religion and spirituality. Religion refers to a "set of beliefs concerning the cause, purpose, and nature of the universe, especially when considered as the creation of a superhuman agency or agencies, usually involving devotional and ritual observances and often containing a moral code for the conduct of human affairs." The word derives from the Latin word *religare*, which means to tie, to bind, or to fasten. In other words, religions are the frameworks which bind or tie communities of believers together. They are only one way to approach God, though.

Being spiritual, on the other hand, refers to "the spirit or soul, as opposed to the physical nature." The soul or spirit is considered to be the animating force of the body, and the Latin word *spiritus* or *spiritu* means breath, so things of the spirit are things that keep us alive and breathing. The animating force of God, or the Supreme Being, is therefore referred to as the "Holy Spirit" because He/She/It is said to breathe us into life itself. When we speak of someone as being a spiritual person, it may or may not have anything at all to do with an organized religion.

Although I belong to an organized religion, when I meditate it is for spiritual reasons that may or may not have anything to do with being Catholic.

All of that being said, what does standing in stillness have to do with being holy? What is holiness anyway? In my view, holiness is a *result* of being whole, not the other way around. When we strive to become whole, we are really trying to be the best people we can be, and that would include things like being loving, generous, joyful, patient, caring for others, and being peaceful, faithful, and kind, as well as being able to feel awe for nature and things that touch us emotionally. Killing, revenge, or hurting others never even cross the minds of people who are trying to become whole, because the vibration of wholeness is a higher state of being than negativity. They are on two different wavelengths.

Holiness, though, also includes attributes such as being devoted to God, prayer, and the ability to feel awe and gratitude for all of creation and life itself. Some would refer to these qualities as being saintly, but as we can see, many of the characteristics of wholeness apply here as well.

A holy person is one who is not caught up in matters of ego, such as how things look from the outside. It doesn't matter how much Biblical study someone may have done, or how she stands or sits or kneels when praying. It is not important to wear the "right" kind of clothing when one prays in order for prayers to be heard. God is not that superficial. It doesn't matter if the person holds her hands together with the fingers pointing straight up, or with folded hands, or indeed if he does anything with his hands at all.

In Old Testament times, Moses needed Aaron to help him hold his hands out to the side for his prayer to be acceptable to God. At least that was the way the Scripture writer interpreted prayer from the way the battle was going. As long as Moses had his arms outstretched, the Israelites were winning, but when he got fatigued and his arms dropped to his sides, then they were losing. So Moses called upon Aaron to help him keep the prescribed prayer posture in order for the Israelites to win over their enemies.

However, other traditions often use other postures. Yoga, for example, arose in ancient India and has practitioners in both Hinduism and Buddhism. Devotees pray by sitting in the lotus position and sometimes putting their hands into different *mudras,* with the fingers on both hands at the same time touching different pulse points to effect healing. This practice is often called "Yoga for the hands," but its purpose is not specifically to become holy. Rather it is used to bring the body and the mind into alignment so that a particular type of healing may occur.

Other prayer postures may include kneeling, especially if the prayer is for forgiveness or supplication; standing with arms outstretched in prayers of praise or adoration or when we want to show that our spirit is open to whatever comes our way. Lying prostrate during some rites, such as the ordination of priests, is used to indicate complete submission to the will of God. In Islam, men sit on a prayer mat with their heads touching the floor.

These positions seem to be part of what is called the Perennial Philosophy, which is common to many religions throughout the world and during most of recorded history. My personal feeling about the ways people sit, stand, or kneel comes from an understanding that people usually have a sort of inborn sense of what is appropriate to use with the Eternal One.

In fact, all we have to do is to watch spectators at a sporting event such as a football game to notice what positions our bodies seem to take naturally. Our team is behind, so we clasp our hands before us in a prayer posture: *Please* let us get a touchdown. Oh, our team just scored! Yay! Our hands are held high above our heads in triumph. Oh, no. Their team just intercepted the ball. Our heads are hung in dejection, or perhaps we are screaming in anger. No one has taught us these postures; we just do them automatically.

However, sometimes the posture one chooses for prayer depends upon the culture and religion of one's birth and training. Since nearly all religions have some form of prayer stance, it may depend on the particular sacred tradition involved. Yogis often sit in the lotus position, which is not used in Christianity, but whether one stands, sits, or kneels may depend on the denomination involved.

When we lived in France I was taken aback at first in Catholic churches because there were often no kneelers. Instead, people regularly stood throughout Mass. In some houses of worship there were individual chairs with high backs and very low seats that could be used for sitting if you were short—they seemed to be too low to sit comfortably. If the chairs were turned the other way they were better for kneeling, except then they were almost too high. Some worshipers simply leaned on the backs of the chairs, so I never really knew how one was supposed to use them.

Does God really care if we stand, or sit, or kneel when we pray? I don't think so, but I know it matters a lot to some people. I personally believe that God isn't especially interested in things like that. Does it matter whether we use pre-written prayers or make up our own words? No. It is not so important what we do as we pray so long as our prayer is sincere. I am sure that what He does *not* want is for us to let our egos get in the way of how we relate to Him.

In the Gospel of Matthew, 6:2, Jesus is quoted as saying that God doesn't want us to play the trumpets loudly in the streets when we give alms to beggars, for example. In fact, Jesus specifically says in Matt. 6:6 that we should go into our room and pray to God in secret. In our day, we probably wouldn't take to the streets with a brass band to announce that we donated to Habitat for Humanity, but we might translate that passage to wanting to see our picture in the newspaper for our charity work. Jesus took the Pharisees to task just for that kind of behavior, because then the action becomes more about the person giving alms than about the rightness of the deed itself.

It's not about how holy we look, but about the purity of our intention to be with God. Otherwise it becomes all about everyone praising us for our piety instead of praising God, the One who is worthy of all praise. Remember that when the Pharisee and the publican were both praying in the synagogue, the one that Jesus said we were to emulate was not the pompous Pharisee but rather the humble publican who stood in the back of the space with his head bowed and who asked for forgiveness. This story appears in Luke 18:9-14.

When I was a young girl there were three sisters in our parish whom I always thought of as the "holy old women." They were nearly always in church at some time during the day, in addition to going to Mass every morning. If I had some reason to be in the church, I might slip in the back, or go up in the choir loft to retrieve some music I had forgotten to take home to practice. There they would be, kneeling or sitting quietly, or sometimes saying the Stations of the Cross, walking from one Station to the next. They never noticed I was there. They were in church to be with God, and they didn't care if anyone else saw them or not. That's not why they were there. It was called "making a visit," which was considered to be one of the things holy people did on a regular basis.

I looked upon these three women, Helen, Agnes, and Marie, as wonderful role models on how to live a good Christian life. I thought that they were every bit as saintly as nuns, even though the common thinking was that those who were in a professed religious life must be holier than lay people simply because they had taken vows. I knew that these three—and many others like them—were also holy people.

In regards to making a visit, the nuns who taught catechism often told us the story of little Jimmy, who dropped into the church every day after school. He never stayed long, only long enough to say a quick prayer: "Hello, Jesus. This is Jimmy. I just wanted to say hi."

One day, so the story goes, Jimmy had a bad accident, and a car hit him on the way home from school, so he didn't get to make his usual visit to church. Bystanders later said, though, that they had distinctly heard a voice saying, "Hello, Jimmy. This is Jesus." This happened as the EMTs were working to save Jimmy's life, but unfortunately, the little boy died on the way to the hospital.

This short tale was always told to encourage us to remember God at every moment of our life, because that way, when it came our time to die, Jesus would be sure to be with us. Now whether this story is true or not is beside the point. When our intention is to be with God every day, I am sure that God is with us whenever we need Him to be.

Holiness is a matter of intention. If I intend to make my whole life a prayer, then I can go about my daily routine without constantly saying prayers. I know that I am always connected to God whether

I am working or playing, driving down the street or planting flowers in my yard.

Prayer is not necessarily only words. It can be doing our normal work, taking care of the kids, teaching, driving a bus, or clerking in a store. If our intention is to make all of what we do be a prayer, then that is what it becomes, and we can truly pray without ceasing, even if we aren't saying a word.

When I was little, one of the first prayers we learned in catechism class was to make a morning offering of the day to God. I always have loved that prayer, because once I have acknowledged that God is the mainstay of my life, and that everything I do is for Him, then I am free to follow my passions for swimming, reading, playing the piano, or daydreaming. I know I am not forgetting God, even if I am doing the laundry or washing dishes.

There is a formal morning offering prayer that we learned, but I have long since forgotten the words. So now I just say something like, "Good morning, God. Thank You for the good night's sleep. I offer You my day. Please bless me and all the people whom I meet today, especially those who need You the most. Amen." Any words will do; it is the intention that counts.

Who are some of the people I look up to and think of as role models? Who do I consider today's holy ones? Strangely enough, or maybe not, considering my life's direction, they aren't all Catholic, or even Christian, but many of them are, such as Pope Francis.

I love Francis' concern for the poor and marginalized people of the world, the children and the elderly, those in prisons and nursing homes, the ones most people forget about. I love that he pays his own hotel bills and dresses as simply as he can, given his high office. No red shoes or ermine-trimmed velvet capes for him! He drives a small, energy-efficient car to drive himself around Rome, and he really tries to emulate his namesake, St. Francis of Assisi.

He is a man of the people, and you can just see how he loves them. I love how he takes the world to task for the ways in which we are harming the environment, and I love that he sometimes shows up at Mass in small working-class parishes with no fanfare, humbly sitting in the back with the rest of the congregation. Of course, when the word gets out that the Pope is present, the crowds show up, just as they must have whenever Jesus was said to be coming to a town.

I appreciate that the Pope is trying to bring the Church into modern times, much as his predecessor St. John XXIII did. He is trying to attract the LGBT community by saying, "If this is how God made them, who am I to judge?" In 2016 he traveled to Sweden, which is mostly Lutheran, to try to bring the two faiths closer in harmony. They even discussed the possibility of each group being allowed to receive Communion in the others' churches.

Imagine that! A Pope who loves his people so much that he wants us to be happy and free to love God in the way that is best for us, not by fitting everyone into the same square box, when our shape might be spiral or even donut-shaped. How refreshing! And how much like the Jesus he serves.

I also love the Dalai Lama. He is always smiling and full of joy. In fact, joy seems to be an attribute of all the people I think are really holy. It has something to do with being centered in ourselves and knowing who we really are. People like this do not care about what others think of them. They are free to be wholly themselves, with no posturing or phoniness, just an authenticity about their own being-ness. We can be ourselves around people like that, because they have first shown us how to do it. Their own authenticity gives us the permission to be the same way in our lives.

The Dalai Lama has said that his only religion is to be kind, and I think that is a very good definition of being holy. If it is love, then it comes from God, no matter what the external religion is. Love is the primary requirement.

Ram Dass, the eminent Harvard psychologist who was originally known as Dr. Richard Alpert, is another such joyful person. Once when I was at one of his talks, he came out onto the stage and sat lotus-style on a chair for a good ten or fifteen minutes, just looking at us and breathing. He was utterly still.

The audience was also still, just waiting, but there was a pulsing quality to the waiting. He—and we—were gathering our collective energy for the evening to come. I'll bet that Jesus stood still before He spoke to the crowds of people who followed Him everywhere as well.

The stillness of Ram Dass is what this whole book is about. It was mesmerizing. But there was also an electricity in the air, a sense of expectancy, of wondering what he would say. Then I finally got it. The stillness *was* the message. When we are calm and serene, we are able to take in the wholeness—the holiness—of everything.

I don't remember what Ram Dass spoke about. I only know that the incident made a profound impression on me. We don't have to be constantly *doing* something. Sometimes it's better to just allow ourselves to be still in the present moment.

There are so many wonderful spiritual writers working today. Here are some of the ones I think are truly wise. They are not necessarily Christian, but they go deep into the perennial wisdom of the ages to speak their truth.

I love the late Wayne Dyer, who wrote many inspirational books during his lifetime. Some of my personal favorites are *The Power of Intention*; *Inspiration; Change Your Thoughts, Change Your Life*; and *I Can See Clearly Now.* I have read each of these books many times, especially when I need some encouragement. His protégé, Anita Moorjani, is also deeply inspirational. Her books, *Dying to be Me*, and *What If This is Heaven*? are clearly written from her heart, and she is a very wise person.

Eckhart Tolle, whose book, *The Power of Now,* is another favorite, as is Deepak Chopra, who has written many books on how to know God. Several that I like are *Quantum Healing*, *The Seven Spiritual Laws of Success*, and *God.* Chopra has a distinctly unique perspective, since he grew up in India in the Hindu tradition but was also educated in Christian schools. Thus he has a slightly different take on religion as opposed to spirituality, which is not specific to any one faith tradition.

Some authors whom I have been reading recently also fall into the category of those who have a lot to say without being overtly Christian. They include Sophy Burnham, whose lovely *A Book of Angels* is one of my favorites, and who also wrote *The Ecstatic Journey* and *The Path of Prayer.* Barbara Brown Taylor is an Episcopal priest whose wise and wonderful book, *Leaving Church,* details her spiritual growth adventure when she decided to follow her spiritual self rather than obeying the rules. She also wrote *An Altar in the World* and *Learning to Walk in the Dark.*

Joan Borysenko is also a well-known author. A partial list of her books includes *Inner Peace, 7 Paths to God,* and *It's Not the End of the World: Developing Resilience in Times of Change for Busy People. Guilt Is the Teacher, Love Is the Lesson* is probably her best well-known work, but there are many others that I have not included here.

The Christian authors I find interesting and compelling are Cynthia Bourgeault, Franciscans Ilia Delio and Richard Rohr, and the Enneagram specialists Don Richard Riso and Russ Hudson. All of these writers have a lot to say when one is pursuing the goal of being a whole and holy person.

Not all of my role models are spiritual authors. Some of them come from very different backgrounds, and their life's work is in the public arena rather than being well-known for their focus on God. Some of these people would never make the daily news, but their devotion to helping others is as Godly as any saint you care to name.

I'm thinking of all the teachers, doctors, nurses, firemen, EMTs, and anyone else who may have made a real difference in the way we look at life. There are heroes such as the folks who donate a kidney to a person whose life may depend on it, and the regular people who are facing illnesses, accidents, or death with poise and grace.

In 2015 Jimmy Carter spoke on TV announcing that his cancer had spread to his brain and his liver, and he didn't know how much longer he had to live. His attitude was what amazed me. He was smiling and excited about the next part of his adventure. He acknowledged that he has lived a life full of blessings and really great experiences with the love of his life, his wife Rosalynn. I was so impressed with his acceptance of whatever comes next. There was no whining about how terrible life is, no "why me?" attitude, only joy and excitement about the future.

As it turned out, a few months after the former President made the announcement about his cancer having returned, he told the Sunday School class which he still teaches even into his 90s that his latest scan showed that the cancer had totally disappeared. With his positive attitude and his total reliance on God's goodness, I wasn't all that surprised that he had been healed.

When my husband was diagnosed with colorectal cancer a few years ago, I was certainly not in as good a place as Jimmy Carter seemed to be. I was full of fear for what the future might hold, and those days were stressful for my husband and me. Fortunately, things have turned out well, but I surely didn't face them with the equanimity and faith that Jimmy Carter showed that day. I don't think it was an act on his part, since two of his most delightful characteristics when he was President were his honesty and his forthrightness.

There are also many saints I admire; we probably all have our own favorite people to emulate. You may not call them saints in your tradition; nonetheless, you will certainly know those who you consider heroes.

I love Hildegard of Bingen (1098-1179) for her moral strength and her ability to speak out for women and the earth at a time when those things were not commonly done. I mentioned her briefly in Chapter 9 in connection with mandalas, but she was such a special model of holiness that she deserves more scrutiny. She was a sort of Superwoman, much like Mother Teresa of Calcutta in our day. Mother Teresa was a world traveler in the 20th century, and Hildegard traveled all over Germany and France as a teacher and preacher when women were supposed to stay home and be meek and mild. They were supposed to have a lot of children, or they could be in a monastery, but women were most decidedly not supposed to advise kings and bishops on proper behavior, all the while writing books and music, tending the sick, and founding two monasteries for her Benedictine sisters.

Hildegard's first convent was at Rupertsberg, where she was the main architect, even going so far as to insist on running water for her nuns, quite an innovation in the 12th century. When that motherhouse had so many sisters that they were outgrowing their space, she built a second monastery across the Rhine River at Eibingen. Even into her 80s she traveled twice a week from one house to the other to make sure that things ran smoothly in both of them. I find it amazing that the trip back and forth required her to hike down Rupert's Mountain to the Rhine, get into her little rowboat and row two miles downstream to Eibingen, and then hike up the hill on that side. Of course, she had to do the whole trip in reverse to get back home. Imagine being able to do that in her late seventies!

Hildegard suffered from ill health her whole life, and for her to accomplished as much as she did was a testament to her indomitable spirit as much as it was to her calling to be holy. She was an authority on stones, animals and birds, herbs, and the universe. I am always amazed to look at one of her mandalas, which clearly shows the earth as being round—three hundred years before Columbus actually made the discovery. How did she know this? It's amazing to contemplate.

I also love Teresa of Avila (1515-1582), another powerful woman who wrote so clearly and with such good humor about her trials in the spiritual life. She is also a wonderful role model of the super-woman mold. In her autobiography, *The Life of Teresa of Jesus,* she confesses that she didn't really want to be a nun at all. She fought it for several years, but her father despaired of making a proper lady of her because she was so wild in her youth. Therefore, he sent her off to the local convent to see if the nuns could do anything with her.

While she was there, she discovered that she loved the way the nuns seemed to have a holy purpose for their lives, and though ultimately she decided to join a different order, the Carmelites, her time with the Ursulines was fruitful for her.

I'm not at all sure she was really as "wicked" as she makes herself out to be. She sounds to me pretty much like a normal teenage girl who loved pretty clothes and having nice skin and hair. She and her sister liked to gossip about boys and their friends, which also seems rather usual, but she chastised herself for being too worldly and despaired of ever becoming holy.

However, something about the nuns' life appealed to her, and a few years later, she entered the convent at Avila, Spain. Even after she was there for a while, she was still not convinced that she should become a nun. Eventually she fell ill, and the sisters sent her back home to her father's house to recover. People thought she was dying, and they brought in the priest to give her the last rites. It took three years before she was well enough to return to Avila.

Both Teresa and Hildegard were really strong, accomplished women whom we would probably call superstars today. They were active and contemplative at the same time, living in the world but not of it. Both of them struggled with ill health all their lives. I respect anyone who can do that and still succeed at so many things. They are my heroes.

St. Peter, the uneducated fisherman and man of action, was not one who used his mind. He never quite knew what Jesus was all about, but he loved him fiercely, even though he didn't stand by his friend when Jesus needed him to be there. See the sections in all four Gospels that deal with Jesus' trial to read about Peter's denial of Jesus. Peter is such an example of what it means to be human that I can easily relate to him. Although he wasn't perfect, he persevered to become one of the most recognizable of the saints of the early Church. I appreciate that we don't have to start out being holy but that Source gives us time to mature and grow.

I love St. John XXIII, another person who was disrespected at first but who became one of the great souls of the 20th century. He saw that the Church had grown stuffy and stagnant, so he decided to let in some fresh air and give the old ways some new growth. He showed us what it is possible to accomplish even when we are old and other people count us out.

And of course, there is Mary Magdalene, the "apostle to the Apostles." She of all Jesus' contemporaries understood His message best. She "got" Him, even when the rest of them were all scratching their heads and saying, "Huh? What did He just say?" Even the term Magdalene attests to who she was, for it means "tower" in Hebrew. She certainly was a tower of strength for the rest of the Apostles, and she remains a towering influence for us today.

I have always had a fondness for the Benedictines, probably because we had them as priests at St. Thomas Aquinas parish in Boulder, Colorado, the church in which my husband and I were married. We have a Benedictine convent northwest of Fort Collins as well, the Abbey of St.Walburga. In 2015 they celebrated their 80th anniversary of the nuns being in Colorado, so they had a big open house at their mountainous retreat.

At their Jubilee Mother Maria-Michael Newe, the abbess, gave a short presentation about their life and the singing of the Hours, which begins with awakening at 4:20 a.m. and continues throughout the day. Someone asked her if it wasn't a difficult life.

"Oh, no," she replied with a twinkle in her eye. "It's our *joy*! We have a real rhythm to our days, in that we sing the Psalms, then we work, then we pray some more, then we work again. Our work is our prayer, and our prayer is our work."

She went on to talk about the way they celebrate Vigils, or Night Prayers. "It's the time of day when we give the cares and troubles of the day over to God for healing throughout the night. We forgive each other for any little slights or arguments that may have come up during the day, then I bless each sister with holy oil, and we wish each other a good night. Visitors who come up here to make retreats often tell us that this is the favorite part of our day."

Just being around this woman made me want to be like her, joyful and serene. She is what holiness looks like, at the same time full of inner stillness while attending to the duties of her normal day's activities. She is a person who understands how to find the sacred in her everyday life. There is a wonderful saying about the spiritual life which goes: Before the ecstasy, the laundry. After the ecstasy, the laundry. And so it is. The two things are not separate.

We have seen some wonderful role models to emulate to get us started on the path to holiness. If you are not Catholic, you probably know of people in your own tradition that you consider to be holy. I am sure though, that while the details may be different, the overall feeling and qualities of holy people would be largely the same or at least very similar.

First of course, is a love for God, or Yahweh, or Allah, or the Lord, or the One, or whatever name you call the Deity. Whatever title you use for Him/Her/It/Them is okay. The name is not the important thing here. Source doesn't care what we call Her. Sometimes our love for Him is so intense that it feels like a yearning, because we think that He is only "out there" somewhere, and we are here. But

God is also within us, as close to us as our breath, which is about as close as you can get to someone on this human plane. *Ruah,* the Hebrew word for Spirit, actually means "breath."

It surprised me to learn that the letters for the word *Yahweh,* which is the way the ancient Hebrews refer to God in the Old Testament, actually cannot be pronounced. Of course, those who speak Hebrew know this already, but it was news to me. The YH and the WH were intended to be breathed, as if by the Spirit, with YH on the inbreath and WH on the outbreath, keeping one's lips open instead of touching together. This simple little meditation can be very powerful.

Whether we are trying to be holy or whole, what qualities do we need? Love, joy, peace, patience, kindness, goodness, faithfulness, generosity, centeredness, moral sureness, care for others, and a deep reverence for our Source have been called the Fruits of the Spirit, as set forth in Galatians 5:22-23. These are the ways you can assess your growth in the Spirit. The traits listed above are also how we can tell if we are acting not from our ego but from our deepest Self.

I should probably address the topic of sin before we go any further. Much has been written about sin and the dangers it costs our soul, but one thing I didn't know until recently was where the word "sin" comes from. It turns out it is a term used in archery.

When the student archer is first learning to hold the bow, and how to sight down to where the target is, it may take many times before he gets it right. Often in the course of learning how to do it properly he will miss not just the bull's-eye but the entire target as well. The arrow may just go sailing off into the trees somewhere, not even close to hitting the mark. It takes a lot of practice to learn to do it properly.

Thus, when the shooter's arrow goes astray, he is said to "sin," or miss the mark. In the same way, when our lives go off course, we are said to sin. Now that doesn't mean that we are horrible people because we made a mistake. It does mean that we probably need to make a correction in some area of our life. It's a learning process, and we can't be expected to get it right all the time.

I have heard it said by many different spiritual authors, however, that God judges us much less harshly than we judge ourselves and others because He understands that *we always act from a point of view that—for us—is what we perceive to be holy,* whether or not it looks like holiness to the rest of the world. Even in the matter of sin, then, it would seem that our intention is key. No wonder we are so often told not to judge others, for we have no way to read another person's mind.

Our sins and mistakes are necessary for our growth, much as little children need to fall down over and over as they are learning to walk. We don't get angry with them, though, when they fall. We just gently help them up and let them try again. Eventually everybody learns how to walk, unless there is a physical impediment that gets in the way. We all must find our own ways to God, and our way need not look like anyone else's.

I have learned that our mistakes can be our biggest teachers, and they help us to become who we are today. How else will we ever learn things like compassion, for example, unless we see how our lack of it affects others? Once we truly understand how our harsh words impact those around us, we are then in a position to change our behavior. We may need to make amends for something we have done that has hurt someone else, but until we recognize that we have injured another person, we are not able to transform ourselves. That is the true meaning of repentance, which actually involves rethinking our past behavior and being sorry for it. If we never regret what we have done, we can never turn our lives around.

We have talked about our actions, but what about our interior life? How does that relate to our progress in growing closer to God? How do we learn to stand still and let God in?

Father Thomas Keating, a Trappist monk who lives and works at The Abbey of St. Benedict in Snowmass, Colorado, re-introduced the ancient practice of Centering Prayer during the 1980s. He wanted the laity to be able to practice this form of contemplation in the same way that monks do, even though many people, priests and monks included, thought that this type of prayer was only for those in monasteries or convents. The laity were not thought to be able to be holy because of the duties of family life.

Father Thomas thought that was nonsense. In the early Church, there was no distinction between the laity and others who wanted to live a life of prayer. If a person wanted to be a hermit, he or she found a cave somewhere and went off alone to be with God. There were no seminaries, no monasteries or convents, so people who wanted to dedicate themselves to God were on their own.

In the 1960s the Beatles traveled to India to learn about meditation because there wasn't any other way to get this kind of instruction. Because many people were put off by what they thought of as "hippie nonsense," Father Thomas created the Contemplative Outreach program as a way to teach Christian meditation to those who found the Hindu system too esoteric for their needs. He taught workshops all around the U.S. to parishes whose congregants wanted to learn this new/old way of praying.

One of the parishes Father Thomas visited was John XXIII in Fort Collins, where I was a member. It was a weekend retreat, and about thirty people gathered to pray and to learn together how to do this "new" spiritual practice. At the time I was very involved with the music ministry, so the idea of interior prayer didn't really speak to me.

Fast forward to December of 2011 when I had the fall that would change my life. As you already know, I was confined to a rehab facility for almost two months, and my injuries were so severe that someone had to help me do the simplest things.

No one told me that the physical therapy and occupational therapy would be over for the day by 8:30 a.m. That left a whole lot of the day empty to do—what, exactly? Sure, my husband was very good about coming around ten o'clock, Starbucks in hand for me, but he often wasn't able to stay all day since he had a house to run and cats to take care of when I wasn't there to do it for him. So I read a lot, but after a few hours of that, my eyes would go buggy. I've never been one to watch daytime TV, and I frankly didn't feel good enough to go out in my wheelchair, what with my right arm in a cast from wrist to elbow, and my other leg in a brace from above my knee to my ankle.

My friends were good about visiting, but they, too, have busy lives and couldn't spend more than a half hour or so cheering me up. And I didn't expect them to.

So I began to meditate, at first as a way to fill the empty hours, and later because I realized how much I enjoyed it. I began to look forward to the time spent in silence just being present to the Presence.

The deepest, darkest part of the night was the most conducive to meditation, and I often used that time as time to center and be still. That was the real start of my meditation practice, and I still continue it years later. There is something about the quiet of the night that is especially fruitful for me, and I understand why monks and nuns rise early to take advantage of this special time to be with God. There is not much else that a person is called to do at 3:00 a.m. other than to spend this fertile darkness germinating, much as a seed does in the rich fecundity of the dark soil. It is a special and a specially blessed time.

Father Thomas talks about how God becomes the Divine Therapist when we meditate a lot. Difficulties or problems that may have been hidden in our psyche for many years, perhaps since childhood, come up for resolution. This is not an easy practice, but it does bear fruit if we stick with it long enough.

The trick here is to allow everything that arises to be welcome and not to try to fight it to make it go away. Our minds will do anything they can to get us to ignore or push down the uncomfortable feelings, but the truth is that when we allow them to arise, more than likely they will last only about ten seconds or so before they dissipate of their own accord. That doesn't mean they won't recur. Of course, they will, many times.

Say I am experiencing violent anger, which is red-hot and burning and makes me want to do harm to myself or another. If I don't attach any story or meaning at all to the anger, just allow it to be here in all its fury, eventually it will wear itself out. We cannot sustain high emotion for very long. It's just not possible, even though we feel as though it's going to consume us when we are in the midst of it. It won't.

Just let it do its thing and then it's over. I always feel enormously better than I would have had I spent the time trying to get it to go away. The emotion wants to be heard. Maybe it's been sitting there in my cells since I was three, and until I give it permission to express itself it will keep showing up as illness or stress somewhere else in my life until it feels safe enough to come out.

Another method of self-discovery that I like a lot is the Enneagram. This is an ancient system that divides all of humanity into nine ego Types, each with their own characteristics, some healthy, some less so. When we begin to identify which Type is the most like us, we begin to understand why we do some of the things we do and why we find ourselves stuck in the same patterns year after year. Once we know our Type we can find a path toward making the necessary corrections, as well as knowing why some of our actions seem to be almost an addiction. We also discover that special graces and gifts go along with each Type, and we can then begin to integrate these so that we experience the balance of a healthy and whole personality.

In Part Two of this book I go into more detail about the Enneagram, but to really get a good handle on what it is all about, I suggest reading the books by Don Richard Riso and Russ Hudson. Their book, *The Wisdom of the Enneagram*, is a classic.

For a more Catholic interpretation of the same material, Richard Rohr and Andreas Ebert have written *The Enneagram: A Christian Perspective.*

Richard Rohr and Russ Hudson gave a joint retreat over the New Year's weekend 2008- 2009 that is now also available on video. This four-DVD set gives an overview of each Type and is very helpful for the beginner to start to understand what the Enneagram is all about. It is called *The Enneagram as a Tool for Your Spiritual Journey: The Laughing and Weeping Conference Recording,* produced for the Center for Action and Contemplation. It can be ordered @caradicalgrace.org, PO Box 12464, Albuquerque, NM 87195. Their phone number is (505)-247-1636.

The late Debbie Ford did a lot of work with the shadow side of our personality, and one of her famous sayings was, "You must own your shadow, or it will own you." We can try to hide the less attractive parts of ourselves, even to the point of denial that they even exist, but sooner or later we have to make peace with them, or they will not let us alone.

Of course it is scary to own up to things we would rather not admit about ourselves; in fact, for most people it is one of the most difficult things we will ever do. But when we finally take that leap of faith and confront our demons we can set them free. We need to embrace our inner self so that we can recognize the games we have been playing with ourselves all our life so that we can let them go once and for all.

When we are working to become holy people, I think it just makes sense to use as many resources as we can to help us find our way. Not every process will be right for every person, because holiness comes in many flavors. We don't all enjoy vanilla ice cream, after all. We just have to find something that will work for us and our particular psychic makeup.

In Part Two I have listed many of the meditations and practices that I have found to be helpful, but the list is not intended to be exhaustive. There are many more self-help books than I know about which can be found in any bookstore or on Amazon, which is a great resource for those who want to use stillness as a way to wholeness/holiness.

CHAPTER 11

Standing in Integrity

We have discussed many of the ways people can stand still during their lives, but one category we have not yet touched upon is how to make our lives mean something. How do we make sure that we stand for something that matters? How do we stay in integrity with who we really are?

What does integrity or acting in integrity even mean?

I'll tell you a story about something that happened to me many years ago that was so strange I have never forgotten it. I was studying at Northern Arizona University, just there for a summer Orff Schulwerk course for three weeks. The Schulwerk is exactly what it sounds like; it is "schoolwork," in this case about how to teach music to children.

Carl Orff was a German composer who lived in the early 20th century. He was already famous when he decided that something needed to be done to help young opera singers, because they stood like sticks on the stage when they performed instead of moving naturally as other actors do. He developed movement classes to help them be more natural onstage, but they still didn't seem to understand how to play in the way that children do as a matter of course, so he added drama classes. Eventually all these improvisational ideas led to an understanding of how children learn, and the Schulwerk was born.

By the time I was studying in Flagstaff the students were already music teachers who taught children. We were looking for a way to revitalize our own teaching and to make it fun for kids at the same time.

The Schulwerk takes percussion instruments that can be played by hand, such as drums, various kinds of shakers and rattles, marimbas which have been cut down to child size with removable bars on them, and glockenspiels—anything that can be hit or struck is fair game. Orff teachers learn to take all the unneeded bars from the instruments so that a child can choose from two or three that all sound good with one another. Using the pentatonic, or five-note scale allows children to be successful, since all the notes—C, D, E, G, and A—work well together.

Orff taught little ones to play the rhythms of familiar nursery rhymes all on the C, then had them make up their own poems. How about adding instrumental accompaniment to the mix?

Would adding a dance or other movement contribute something even more special? Perhaps another type of instrument, such as a recorder, which is a small flute, would make the piece even more interesting. The whole trick to making the piece work is to give the students only a couple of choices in each case, so that they can never be wrong. Too much freedom is only confusing at this young stage of learning.

By the time I was in the second or third week of doing this kind of thing every day, all day, from 8:30 to 5:00, I was totally in love with this creative and innovative way of teaching. There was so much freedom for the teacher to be creative, not to mention how much fun it was. I was totally consumed by it.

I remember crossing the campus one afternoon after classes were finished for the day, and I had a flash of inspiration. THIS is what all my music, dance, and drama classes had been preparing me for all of my life. THIS is why I had always loved to write little songs and poems. THIS is what I was always meant to be doing. I was intended all along to be here in this place, with these people who shared my passion for creative thinking and expression. It may not have been as impressive as the conversion Saul experienced on the road to Damascus (Acts 9:1-9), but it was pretty awe-inspiring all the same.

For me to be a wholly integrated person, I had to follow this path, this new way of being. It was one of the peak experiences of my life. It changed the way I taught—it changed the way I looked at life—forever. Just think, now I would get paid every month for playing all day with kids. How great was that!

In addition, I discovered that my three major professors, all of whom became my good friends during the course of my studies, were also quite spiritual people who were open to a number of things that had nothing to do with music and everything to do with living a whole and centered life. These three lovely women, Liz Gilpatrick, Grace Nash, and Judith Cole, as well as many others whom I met later in my Orff career, showed me that reverence for the sacred could and did play a large part in their daily lives, not just in the music classroom. All of them understood how to live authentically, showing class and grace in doing so.

These women were not Catholic, they were not even necessarily religious, but they lived the *via creativa* to the fullest. The sacred showed up in the way they treated their students and the respect they had for everyone, regardless of nationality, gender, or belief system, if any. We students always knew they loved us and that we could trust them to treat us with dignity and kindness. They lived in in integrity and demonstrated for us how do to it ourselves. That was as least as important as any music lesson they taught.

I will never forget that one year Grace had a Japanese student in her class, and since I knew that she had spent time in a Japanese concentration camp during World War II, I asked her how she could always be so kind to this young man. "Well," she replied, "He wasn't even born when the War happened, so how could I treat him poorly? He is as deserving as anyone else of my respect." Very classy response.

For me, my personal integrity is key, but it hasn't always been that way. I didn't always even know what that word meant, much less how to make it a part of my life.

When I was growing up I cared very much for what other people thought about me. I wanted so badly to fit in with my peers that I became a slave to saying, doing things and looking the way I thought others wanted me to talk, act, and dress. It never occurred to me that I could follow my own star, and indeed would have to do just that if I ever wanted to be a fully functioning adult. It is a normal growth pattern for teens as they try to separate from their parents and the parental rules, but the problem comes when people carry these teenage ideas into adulthood, often because they don't know that they can choose to live their lives a different way.

Even St. Paul says, "When I was a child, I thought as a child, I spoke as a child, I reasoned like a child. But when I became a man I put away childish things." (1 Cor.13:11). Good old St. Paul. He was a wise man and he understood human nature.

When we are small, we tend to reflect the beliefs and ideas we hear at home and at school. But when we grow up and leave home, we see something of the wider world, and we begin to realize that the way we have always thought about things and done things are not the only possibilities open to us. So it makes sense that as our ideas grow and change, so too do we adapt stances that may be at odds with those of our birth families.

I once had a student, a lovely and thoughtful girl, who was having a dilemma with her grandmother, who wanted Traci (not her real name) to major in a subject that was not at all what Traci wanted for herself. Yet she loved her grandmother dearly and wanted to earn her approval. What should she do?

After I had spent some time with the girl, I told her what I would tell any young person in the same situation. "You are not your grandmother. She had certain goals for her life, and that was the way she lived. Now it's your turn to live your own life, not your grandmother's. Your grandmother did what she felt was right for her; now you must do the same. If she truly wants what is best for you, she will come around. If she doesn't, your life is still *your* life, not hers."

I was lucky enough to have parents who supported me in my career goals and to be whoever and whatever I chose to be. I know many teenagers don't have that kind of support, though. It can be very difficult to go against familial expectations, but in the end we must each follow our own path, and no one else can choose that for us.

Not only is it not easy to go against the wishes of our family, sometimes we don't even know that we *can* make our own choices. I was probably in my forties before someone pointed out to me that I could make my own decisions and that we *always* have a choice in the matter.

I remember what a shock it was to hear that revelation. "You mean I get to choose what my life looks like?" I recall being astounded at that thought, which I had never heard before. My family lived by the rules of society and the church; choice never entered into it. You did what you were told. Yet here was this world-famous clinician saying that I am my own best expert. No one else. *Me.* I get to choose it, all of it. Huh. Wow!

I have to admit, though, that when I embarked on the study of Orff Shulwerk, my mother had a hard time accepting my new way of doing things. I'm sure she thought I had totally flipped my lid, because even though she loved dancing, music, and having fun, the concept of having fun at work was something she could not comprehend. Her life, like so many of her generation, was more about doing your duty to your family and your church. Fun didn't enter into the equation; you just did what you had to do and didn't complain about it. It was simply the way life was.

In the 1950s, the idea for women's lives, especially in a largely German-Irish community like the one I grew up in, was "Kinder, Kirchen, and Kuchen." Children, church, and cooking. My mother had already stepped outside of those boundaries when she got a job in our local flour mill as a secretary to the vice president of the corporation during World War II. She was the only mom I knew who worked outside the home, and it was only possible for her because Grandma was home all day to take care of me. Otherwise, my mother was a very traditional, conservative Catholic woman of her time, so my wanting a job that was fun was totally unheard of for her. Her own work experience had been that people worked to pay the bills, not because it was enjoyable.

We talked a little earlier about thinking of things in terms of saying "Yes" to life rather than "No." Saying "Yes" implies that we are open to possibilities, rather than just going along with the crowd, and of taking chances to make our lives mean something rather than just coasting along being passive. However, first we sometimes have to overcome ideas that we learned as children which now don't serve us very well.

I am thinking about concepts such as "A quitter never wins, and a winner never quits," "Someone who changes his or her mind is a waffler," or "Always stay the course." A lot of people would never think to question these mottos or understand that they work in some situations, but not in everything we do.

Of course, those ideas can be good sometimes, but for every time they are the right answer, there are probably at least as many times when they would be absolutely the wrong way to proceed. If you are dealing with a problem that must be solved, you must certainly stay with it until you figure out a solution. However, if your dream is to become an Olympic gold medalist but you decide to quit halfway through your training, you can be sure you will never win a gold medal. You have to know when quitting serves you better than sticking out the course you have set for yourself.

I'm thinking of a job I had one time that I really, really hated. I was still using the "quitters never win" model of behavior, so I stuck it out for far longer than I should have, because I was miserable in the position. I probably should have left at least a year earlier than I did, but I didn't want to be seen as a quitter, so I stayed. In retrospect, that was a dumb thing to do, but I learned a good lesson from it. I learned what I *didn't* want, and that is at least as valuable as knowing what it is that I *did* want.

Learning to stand up for ourselves is not easy, and many of us don't realize that we can choose to make of our lives what we want them to look like. In fact, if we want to live in integrity, we must do it.

Of course, I knew I could make some choices for myself. I didn't need anyone's permission to choose my clothes, or what guy I should marry, or where and when I should get higher education. Those things were fairly easy. But I thought I needed someone with more experience or more knowledge than I had to figure it all out for me when it came to God and things of the spirit. We Catholics are not used to making our own choices spiritually.

Nowadays whenever I need to make a decision, I understand that I may need to take some time to stand still and ponder which course is right for me. I also see that I am the one who is responsible, so I don't get to blame anyone else if things go wrong. The one thing that is the underpinning of my whole life is, am I in alignment with who I really am? Am I standing in integrity with my soul's purpose for my life? If I am, then whatever I choose will be the right thing for me.

However, when I first heard the concept about making my own choices as they related to my own integrity, I hardly understood what that meant. I wasn't even sure what integrity was, exactly. Or even inexactly.

What was the thing that made me *me?*

After I retired from teaching, I discovered that what I am doing now is different both in intention and in content from what I had done earlier in my life. In the first part of our lives we are busy building our family, our career, and learning about who we are in this world and how we relate to others. That process is a necessary under-layer that we must have in place before we can even attempt to do the work of the second half of life.

Recently Father William Meninger, a Trappist monk who lives at the Abbey of St. Benedict in Snowmass, Colorado, was here in Fort Collins giving a two-day retreat for the people of my parish. He agreed that the first half of our lives sets the foundation for doing the work that we are called upon to do as we age. Laughing, he looked around at the group who had assembled to hear his talk on St. John of the Cross, a 16th-century Carmelite Spanish monk, saying to us, "Aha! Just as I thought! There's hardly anyone here who is under the age of forty. That is as it should be. Younger people have not lived enough to understand what I'm going to talk about in this lecture."

His topic was St. John's seminal work, *The Ascent of Mount Carmel*. In this book, John spells out the ways the soul ascends to God throughout its lifetime, from starting at the very beginning at the foot of the mountain to gradually climbing all the way to the very top, which is where the soul finally experiences complete union with the Divine, without words, without any of the ego fixations that we all have in earlier stages. For most people, this is the work of a lifetime, and for some, the top is only reached on one's deathbed. For others, unless they are really on a spiritual path for their whole life, they may never reach this stage at all.

The reason this is referred to as the work of the second half of life is that once the children are grown, and we have retired from the busy life we have always known before, there is time to stand still and contemplate what it all means. People who are in their 20s and 30s simply haven't had enough experience to make sense of it all.

Father William, who has long been the novice master at St. Benedict's Abbey, said that sometimes young men enter the monastery with a copy of John of the Cross's books in their hands, hoping to make a good impression. "Know what I tell them?" he asked, his eyes twinkling. "I tell them to burn the book! They are not old enough to read it."

I could certainly relate to what Father William was saying. I remember having to read John of the Cross's *Dark Night of the Soul* in my junior or senior year in Theology class at Marymount College. It made absolutely no sense to me at all. I couldn't understand what a 16th century Spanish mystic had to say about living through deep feelings of being abandoned by God. I was about twenty at the time and in the midst of a torrid love affair, so being unloved was not something high on my list of problems. I was much more concerned with when I would see my boyfriend again, not being abandoned.

While I found it hard to relate to John of the Cross, St. Teresa of Avila is another of those 16th-century Spanish mystics whose works endure to this day, and she is far easier to read. In her book about the spiritual path, *The Interior Castle,* she compares the way we approach prayer to entering a beautiful castle which has many rooms.

When we are first out in the courtyard, before we start to enter the spiritual life, we encounter many bugs, snakes, lizards, toads, spiders, and other beasties that live outside the castle. As we progress into the first level, we may still have some of those things on us or around us. They don't belong inside the castle, but we bring them in on our clothing or in our hair.

Teresa likens these creatures to the things of the world that are unimportant or which will hinder us as we progress spiritually. They may also be attitudes or even sins that we have carried around with us for as long as we can remember.

In my experience, they may also be vows that we have made to ourselves at some point that may have been important at one time but now no longer serve us. I am thinking of things such as, I will never (or always)_____________(insert your vow here). If I am ten years old and hate boys, then I might vow never to get married, but if I am 26, deeply in love and sure that I have met the man that I intend to marry, that vow makes no sense. I have outgrown the promise I made to myself, but the energetic quality of that pledge is still stuck in my cells. It's time to let it go.

Gradually, as we ascend higher and higher into the more and more beautiful rooms of Teresa's castle, we find that most of those worldly concerns (bugs, and other dirt we have carried inside with us) begin to drop off. They no longer concern us. In the final stage, just as John of the Cross wrote in his book, there is nothing left but God alone. We are simply in union with Him. While most of us will probably not experience as much of the union as these two great saints did, I have had brief moments of sinking into the Presence of something holy. It only lasted for a couple of seconds, and afterwards I am never sure if it really happened. However, this theme of union is common among spiritual writers, so it must be true. They can't all be making it up.

During their lifetimes, Teresa and John were close friends and associates, united in their work of reforming the Carmelite orders for men and women, which had become quite corrupt and un-spiritual in the way their monasteries were run. In those days in Spain, a woman would have had a hard time getting support for her work of returning her convent to the spiritual place it was meant to be. Instead, many convents had become dumping grounds for the younger daughters of noble families who couldn't make suitable marriages for them. These girls, some quite young themselves, probably wouldn't have had anything to say about their choices for their lives, instead being shuttled off to live in a convent along with all their servants, pets, and hangers-on. They were certainly not there to learn to live a saintly life. But it solved the problem of what to do with younger daughters for those families who might not have been wealthy enough to provide a proper dowry for them.

So St. Teresa was in a bind. She needed a male benefactor to help her with the politics of what she was proposing to do, which was to return the Carmelites to their former state, namely that of being a house of prayer. You can imagine that she got a lot of resistance from those who were already in her convent, since they quite liked the life of luxury that they were leading.

She prayed long and hard to find such a champion, when, quite by accident, she met John on the road after one of their carriages had overturned in a creek, and he and his companions were trying to extricate themselves from the situation. During the ensuing hours of getting the conveyance back on the road, she and John struck up a conversation, and they realized that they were both Carmelites, and that they shared similar ideas about reforming their motherhouses.

Now John was a tiny little man, barely reaching five feet tall, whereas Teresa cut a rather more imposing figure. Also, she was 67, and he was in his twenties. None-theless, they were cut from the same cloth spiritually, and they became allies.

Afterwards, Teresa always joked that she had prayed for a man to help her reach her goals, but that God had seen fit to send her "only half a man." John may have indeed been short, but he was a spiritual giant.

Now these two great saints certainly understood integrity. They knew what their great work was to be, and they became partners in seeing it to fruition. They were passionate about what they were doing, and eventually they accomplished their life's work.

In addition, at the time that they were reforming the Carmelites, the Spanish Inquisition was at its full height, going after anyone they suspected of being a heretic, so both Teresa and John were very careful in what they said and did so as not to anger the authorities. Those who went against the powerful could easily find themselves on trial for their very lives. While Teresa and John made sure that they were in integrity with what the Catholic Church thought and taught at the time, they were in integrity with themselves as well.

What about us? How do we know if we are in integrity with ourselves or not?

Like so much of this book, the answer lies in how we feel about our work. Does it make us happy? Are we fulfilled by what we do? Do we have a passion for our work? Do we enjoy it, or do we simply slog through it day by day, just waiting for the weekend?

If we can answer yes to being joyful about what we do, more than likely we have found what we are supposed to be doing with our life. If, on the other hand, we find ourselves hating our boss and our co-workers and dreading Monday mornings, then maybe we need to take a good hard look at our job and take some standing still time to see if there might be something else that would suit us better.

Integrity usually refers to "being whole, complete, at one with oneself" and who we know we are. Thus if we are doing work that doesn't make us feel whole, or if we are in a relationship in which we have to hide parts of ourselves to get along, we are probably not in integrity with who we are. When we are in integrity with ourselves, everything just seems to fit. Everything has a rightness to it that doesn't need any explanations. We don't have to hide any part of ourselves.

By contrast, when we are not in integrity we feel like something is missing or out of place with our lives. If we have to keep telling lies to make ourselves believe that everything is okay, then we are probably not in integrity. We know it when we feel whole and right. We don't have to make excuses or rationalize our behavior. We are right on target, to return to the image of archery. The bull's-eye is within reach of our arrows.

All of us grow up with questions about our lives, and those questions will probably change as we move from one stage of our lives to another.

I have a dear friend who is a priest in the Ecumenical Catholic Communion, which allows women to serve in this way. She is wise and compassionate, and when she teaches her middle school Confirmation classes, she has the students write out their own creeds. She explains that in the early days of the Church, the people who wrote the Nicene and Apostles' creeds were searching for a way to set down what they believed, just as these modern-day teens are.

I was astounded by the depth and breadth of their finished creeds. They tackled things like caring for the earth and compassion for animals, as well as more traditional spiritual beliefs. They recognized that there are many types of world religions and that most of them have at least some truths in them, regardless of whether they are Christian or not. They understand that God has no gender and doesn't play favorites with one group of people over another. I was very impressed that these young people came up with such genuine and well-thought-out ideas.

What things do you believe? Not what does some Who-Said-of-the-Greatest-Magnitude say you "must" believe if you want to go to heaven, but what is really important to you? Your beliefs may or may not have anything at all to do with formal religion. If you are really in line with your own integrity, what do you choose for yourself? We all have beliefs about many things, not just the spiritual life.

Years ago I took a course of study in a psychospiritual discipline called The Journey. This is a program developed by a woman named Brandon Bays for discovering the obstacles that keep us bound up instead of free. As a person works his or her way through the classes, which usually takes several years of training, one roots out vows we may have made to ourselves, beliefs we have about the world, and the like. There are seminars about the Enneagram, which I talked about briefly in the previous chapter. The Enneagram is an ancient device that divides all human behaviors into nine distinct types. We learned about our own types, and why we all behave the way we do because of our particular ego fixation. It was very liberating for me to understand what has been driving my fears all these years, for example, and why I can never seem to get completely rid of them.

The Journey is not for the faint of heart. Some of the processes we did are extremely difficult and taxing, yet there is nothing better for learning who we really are. There were times when we felt awful, as well as times of high elation. It's a roller coaster ride, for sure, but the results are so beneficial that we were all willing to go through the difficult times to get to a place of more freedom. In fact, when we had all done a particularly difficult day in which we had done two or three processes in just a few hours, we were said to have "Journey eyes," which meant that other people noticed how we were glowing from having let go of so much old "stuff." St. Teresa of Avila called these the dirty, beast-like parts of ourselves that keep us from being all that we are meant to be.

Earlier I mentioned doing a process of journaling when you bump up against a problem or difficulty in your life. I think journaling is a powerful tool to use, because somehow the act of putting things down on paper seems to come from a different—and deeper—place in ourselves than we usually are able to access. If you don't have access to The Journey or some other intense and profound way of rooting out some of these hidden and incorrigible problems, journaling may be a way of getting to the heart of the difficulty.

One of the questions I like to ask myself for reflection is "Who Am I?" I noticed that when I began doing this process many years ago, my answers would be things like: I am a teacher, a wife, an American, and other similarly superficial attributes. Or sometimes the responses would be things like: I am tall. I am blonde. (Well, that was then!) I have green eyes. All these things were true, but they didn't go very deep, because I had not yet learned to access that interior place in myself.

There is another, similar process of unmasking hidden trouble spots. I learned it in a workshop many years ago, and I still find it to be useful. It can be done either alone or with two people, one of whom answers the other's question, "What masks are you wearing if you take a staircase or elevator one level below the surface?" The first level is still fairly superficial, so you may not even be aware of a mask at all. Again, my answers were mostly on the surface. It took me until about the fourth or fifth level below until I noticed I was wearing a mask; from then on down until about Level 10, the masks got uglier and more evil-looking. Then the answers became, "I am a bully. I am a liar. I hide my real self behind the mask of needing other people's approval." This area was similar to the outer courtyard of St. Teresa's castle that was mentioned earlier, full of nasty stuff.

I became aware that the things I was hiding from myself and others lurked deep in my subconscious. Most of us are not usually enlightened enough to recognize these things unless we make a conscious effort to "unmask" them. We have to notice these behaviors before we can correct them, and the observation isn't always fun, but it must be done if we really want to be in integrity with our true Self.

I have described doing this exercise with someone else, but if no one is around to help you do this process, you can certainly journal it as well. The thing I have noticed about journaling is that sometimes your pen writes something you didn't know you thought or believed. For this reason, I recommend that you actually use a pen rather than a tablet or a computer, because there is some sort of neurological connection that is made by the action of actually physically doing the writing rather than using a mechanical device. You won't get the same results from a computer that your hand gets. Your intention here is to clarify what exactly you are thinking about a problem or difficulty, and it may not be at all what your waking brain assumes it is.

Another, more difficult way of doing this same exercise is to use your non-dominant hand to do the writing. Talk about bringing up old "stuff!" Writing this way will access a lot of old childhood memories you have probably forgotten that you had.

Even when I use my dominant hand, sometimes I have also been able to uncover a vow that I didn't know I had made, perhaps years before and which now no longer serves me. If that is the case, then I call upon an angel or spirit guide to come help me wash it out, or vacuum it up, or dissolve it into harmless sparkling light that can then dissipate harmlessly into the atmosphere.

Think, for instance, of Jacob Marley's chains in *A Christmas Carol* and how those links held him back in his life. Those are the kinds of things I am talking about here. Marley was no longer able to do anything about his bonds, but his friend Ebenezer Scrooge had the opportunity to let his shackles go and to live a freer and more integrated life. I, for one, want to remove as many obstacles to living in God's love as I possibly can, right now, while I still have the time to do something about them.

Another way of knowing our inner selves is to look at what are called Archetypes. These may be The Warrior, The Teacher, The Entertainer, The Communicator, The Hero, and The Policeman. There are many others. If you look at yourself honestly, to what quality or type of job do you seem to always gravitate? Are you an Earth Mother? A Saint? A Mediator? Are you always trying to help others, or are you more drawn to being a painter or a builder? Are you someone who is always reliable and the one that everyone else turns to in times of difficulties? Or do you bury your head in books, trying to learn everything you can about a particular subject? These types of questions can help you decide which qualities are your special interests.

For example, I have always been pulled to teach, and I've been doing it in one form or another all my life. I started teaching swimming lessons and piano lessons when I was 14, and I have always taught something, whether it was public school music, or leading a dance troupe, or teaching catechism to 5th graders. I've taught kindergarten through college level courses, as well as seminars teaching teachers how to teach. So The Teacher is probably my main archetype.

But I am also a Communicator, because I have been writing and composing music all my life as well. When I was ten I wrote my first play, which the neighborhood kids then performed in our neighbors' driveway, where we set up folding chairs and charged our parents a penny to get in. That same mom was my first editor and critic, and she encouraged me to keep writing. I wrote stories that I used in my music classroom, and I've written the music that accompanied them. I wrote a Mass when I was doing a Master Class in Orff Schulwerk, with the late great Orff teacher, Grace Nash, as my major professor.

All of these things I tell you, not to toot my own horn so much as to help you see that all along I have been acting in integrity with my natural abilities. I didn't always know that's what I was doing, but now that I think about it, I can see that it was an inborn God-given sense of being on my own special path.

No doubt, once you begin to think about it, you will notice such patterns in your own life.

Who are the people who embody integrity for us?

Well, Jesus is the most obvious answer for Christians, since He was willing to give up everything His ego thought He wanted in order to do the Father's will, even when He understood it meant He would have to suffer and die. But He is not our only exemplar.

Martin Luther King was another such soul. He also knew that by living the life he did, by standing up for justice for African Americans, that there were other people who would hate him for taking such a brave stance. He understood, as Jesus did, that he probably would have to forfeit his life to stay true to his own principles. Neither he nor Jesus *wanted* to die, but they were both willing to do so in order to stay in integrity with themselves.

The young Pakistani girl, Malala Yousafzai, is another such brave person. She has told her story in her book, *I Am Malala: The Girl Who Stood Up for Education and Was Shot by the Taliban.* She knows that they may try again to kill her, but she has said repeatedly that she would die rather than to stay silent. She knows that girls deserve to be educated, but she also knows that many men around the world feel very threatened by smart women. She is quite aware of having a price on her head for her beliefs, but she is living in her own integrity.

Most of us will probably never be called upon to face being martyred for our beliefs. However, there are more subtle things that challenge us to live up to our own sense of wholeness: The teenager who is being pressured to use drugs or alcohol when she doesn't want to use them, but she feels like she has to in order to stay part of her social group. The worker at a company who is asked to sign off on a product that doesn't meet safety standards but the boss is in a hurry to get it on the market quickly so as to beat a rival company. When we are asked to lie or cover something up for a friend or co-worker. These are some examples of what it means to face threats to our own sense of who we are.

How we deal with such things speaks a lot about what kind of character we have. If we knuckle under and lie for expediency's sake, if we engage in risky behavior just to be "one of the gang," or if we compromise the safety of a product that we know could cause injury or death to another, all these things affect our integrity.

Even if we rationalize such behavior to ourselves by saying, "Oh, it's only this one time. It'll never happen again," or "It's just the way we do business," we have set a pattern for ourselves. Since we did it once, it will be easier the second time, and the third, until finally we don't even notice that we have sold our soul for thirty pieces of silver. It just becomes our normal way of doing things. Before we know it, we have lost our integrity.

For me, my soul is my most prized possession, the "pearl of great price," (Matt. 13:45) and I don't want to let anyone else tell me what I may or may not believe or how I should act. I think I am finally beginning to understand the saying, "For what does it profit a man if he gains the whole world but loses his soul in the process?" (Mark 8:36)

I am not completely there yet. I know there is still a lot of emotional baggage to let go of, not just for me, but for all of us. As long as we are on this planet, undoubtedly there will be things that we still need to forgive and to make complete. As a friend says, "We can never get it wrong, and we can never get it finished." There will always be more to do. However, the good news is that God still loves us, no matter how much "old stuff" we still carry around. As many great sages have said throughout the centuries, "All paths lead to God, for where else is the soul to go?" I find that thought very comforting.

There was a time when I would have questioned anything that came from a source other than the Catholic Church, but I have discovered that no particular church or religion has cornered the market on the truth. Truth is what it is, no matter where it comes from. This realization even has a name: The Perennial Philosophy, which is true in all times and cultures, no matter where in the world they are or at what time in history.

The wonderful St. Thomas Aquinas, who is a Doctor of the Church, which means that he is considered to be very advanced spiritually, once said, "Don't worry about who has said something. If it's true, you will know that it came from the Holy Spirit." That means that it is not true just for one religion or culture, or in one generation but not another, but that *even in spiritual matters we cannot get it wrong.*

The English poet Francis Thompson (1859-1907) says that God will keep reaching out to us wherever we are in our lives, like "the hound of heaven." God wants us to be with Him, however we are, whoever we are. He will never stop trying to gather us to Himself. He will pursue us to the ends of the earth, and until the ends of our lives, as my friend Denise says, "like a puppy that just won't leave you alone but keeps panting after you, just waiting for you to notice him."

Our quest to find ourselves is the job of a lifetime. What an exciting job it is! Nothing is more thrilling than finding out who we really are. It's like coming home to what we always knew but never recognized before.

When we finally "get" who we are intended to be, and who we always have been, then it's easier for us to live in integrity, because we don't want to dishonor God's creation. We *want* to be fully ourselves. In fact, it would be very uncomfortable for us *not* to live in as integrated a way as we possibly can, all the days of our lives. Standing in integrity means showing up in our lives as the person we were always meant to be.

CHAPTER 12

Standing in the Presence of Mystery

When we have come to the end of our life, it seems that for many of us it is the scariest time of our whole existence on earth.

Much of our culture seems to be averse to the idea of talking about death, or even recognizing that it exists, in some cases. Think about it. We so often tuck our dying relatives into nursing homes or hospitals, out of sight, and often out of mind. We avoid talking about the subject, often to the point of telling the dying ones that they will soon get well, when we know in our heart of hearts that such an outcome is unrealistic.

If someone has reached the age of ninety, has trouble with seeing, hearing, and walking, and may not even recognize the family members who were once so well-loved, we must come to terms with the idea that death is probably imminent for that person, as uncomfortable as that realization may make us.

In olden times, the dying one was well looked after by the family, who understood that death is simply a part of the natural way of things. It is perhaps easier to see that when you live closer to nature than modern people do. It was not uncommon for ancient tribe members to have lost a child to disease, to accidents, or to other events completely out of the parents' control. They could possibly rant and rave at the unfairness of it all, but when it came right down to it, death was seen as a natural ending to life. Existence itself was not a given; people routinely died at thirty or so, and they just accepted it as a part of the way things were.

If a tribe was used to killing animals for food, as Native Americans once did, the people understood that death comes to everyone and every being that lives, from animals to plants to human beings. These early people lived in small groups who were close to the earth, and they saw the passage of the seasons and the dying of trees and other plants. They killed animals for food, not for sport, and they used every part of the body for something. The hide could be tanned for clothing or to make the outside of the tepee; the fur of a buffalo or bear could be worn as a cloak to keep out the cold or for bedding inside the home. As a result of this interdependence of humans and animals, the hunters thanked an animal before they shot it, and they looked upon it with reverence for shedding its life to feed and clothe them. Death then was honored for its place in the grand scheme of things.

However, in our modern world, we have conquered so many diseases that we forget that life is not intended to be a forever thing, at least not on this planet. Doctors often seem to treat death as though it is the enemy, when for many people who are suffering and in terrible pain, it comes as a release.

So why are we so afraid?

I think many people would say that the fear of death is the most basic, primary terror there is, because we have no idea what really comes next, and the unknown is always scary.

Life on this planet seems to have developed to help us to grow and evolve throughout the time we are alive. This book is called *Standing Still*, and yet, standing still is the one thing we really cannot do on earth. Our very purpose is to change. If we look at any species, plant or animal, we see that there are stages of growth for them all. There may be a seed, as for plants, which then matures into a flower, or a food crop, or a tree, but it doesn't stand still. It can't. Everything evolves into whatever its next stage is going to be.

Whether with animals, insects, birds, fish, or humans, we all start out in one form and then become something else. A caterpillar morphs into a beautiful butterfly, a tadpole becomes an adult frog, an egg hatches into a chicken, duck, or other bird.

With humans it is the same thing. We don't start out fully grown; we are first an embryo, then a baby, then a toddler, a teenager, an adult, and finally an old person nearing the end of life. Of course, things don't always follow the normal pattern; some children die as toddlers, and some adults live to be 100. An accident may take the life of a promising teen just getting started in life. The one constant is that all of us face departing from Earth at some point.

So why is that so terrifying for us?

Part of it is, I think, that we have no idea what comes next. Our religions may tell us there is an afterlife, but no one has ever returned to tell us exactly what that means. We may talk about heaven or hell as though we have some concept of what those terms mean, but the truth is that we have no real idea. Just because some Who-Said-of-the-Greatest-Magnitude says it is so doesn't make it true.

Nonetheless, almost every culture on the planet has some version of what comes next. Just how that is to play out will differ from country to country and religion to religion.

I like the idea Father Thomas Keating has about the afterlife, which he talked about in a video on death and dying that was filmed at the Abbey in Snowmass. For him, the way we think and feel on earth is also the way we will feel after we die. The whole thing is a continuum for him. If we embrace life and love as fully as we can, we are already in heaven, but if we hate everything and everyone around us, we probably won't change all that much when we die.

So for Father Thomas, we are in heaven or hell for the greatest part of our lives, just by the way we live.

He goes on to say that he likens death to a change in state, much like when we are *in utero* and that is the only form of life that we know. It's generally a comfortable, warm, nourishing place where all our needs are taken care of, so when we are what we call "born," we are suddenly thrust into a cold, big area where we are expected to breathe air for the first time. It must come as something of a shock to our systems. Then we find out that this world is not so bad.

However, regardless of the circumstances of our lives, death is going to find us all eventually. At that point, Father Thomas says that we will once again find ourselves in a new situation, although not an unpleasant one if we have lived a life of loving others throughout our time on earth. It will be different, to be sure, because we will not have sure knowledge of the details before we make our transition, but we will still find ourselves surrounded by love and possibly the people we knew on this planet.

Even the late, great saint, Pope John Paul II talked about heaven and hell as being primarily states of consciousness. It has to do with being present to what is around us right now. The now is all that we ever get, so being present to what is going on for us at this moment can be either heaven or hell, depending on how we look at it.

Even the Psalmist hints at heaven as being at least partially on earth, for as he writes in Psalm 27, "I remain confident of this: I will see the goodness of the Lord in the land of the living." (NIV) That to me that is another way of saying that heaven is here on earth for those who are willing to see it. If we believe that God is love, and we live our lives as loving people, then we are united with God, even if we don't call it heaven.

Therefore, the process for finding God seems to be nothing more or less than letting ourselves be open to our version of the divine, whatever that might be.

Oprah Winfrey produced a series of shows that aired recently on her network, OWN, that is called simply *Belief.* It follows a number of different kinds of religions and traditions throughout the world and the beliefs that each one subscribes to. The people are not all religious, but they are all spiritual in their own way.

One of the people she highlights is a rock climber who undertakes terrifying ascents up the sheerest of rock cliffs without benefit of a harness or other safety equipment. He is not a believer. In fact, he's an atheist. But when she asked him what he imagines when he thinks about death, he said, "Well, I suppose I will have about four seconds of absolute terror if I fall, and then it will be all over. I won't know anything else."

Somehow that doesn't seem so bad. I assume it would be kind of like the way we feel when the anesthesiologist puts us under during surgery. They may have us count down backward from 100, but by about 97 or so, everything just goes completely black, and we don't usually remember anything else until we wake up in the recovery room several hours later.

So why does the whole idea of death scare us so?

I think it is possible that we fear that we somehow won't measure up, and that God will judge us to be wanting. However, I believe that God doesn't judge us in that way, because He gave us all different talents and gifts. I don't think He intended that life should be a competition like *Dancing with the Stars* or *Survivor.* I think God *wants* us to be with Him, and to that end, He is more likely to assess us by how *we* think we are doing, rather than to hold us to some impossibly arbitrary standard. What were the attitudes and beliefs that led us to act in a certain way? I think that compassionate love is the way the Divine One sees us, not as terrible people who made all kinds of mistakes during our lives.

We are so used to everything being a competition, whether it's a football game or a singing or dance contest where everyone is eliminated except for the "best" one, that the idea that everyone deserves to be heard is a novel idea. Everything does not have to be judged by who is the best at whatever the "game" is. Those judgments are a human invention, and I am not at all sure that God operates from the same standard as we do.

Now I am not trying to make myself out to be a saint; far from it. I love my NFL football just as much as anyone else does, and I am probably the one cheering the loudest when my Denver Broncos score a touchdown or the quarterback throws a beautiful spiral down the field for seventy yards. But I recognize that the fun of a sporting event or other kind of competition is on an altogether different wavelength from our relationship with the Divine.

It all comes down to respect for the other. Not just tolerance, because that implies that I am condescending to like you *even though* you are clearly not as good as I am. No. I am talking about loving people because they have their own innate dignity and worth, regardless of who they are. We Christians have learned from Jesus to call God "Our Father," which means that we are all children of God. That alone makes us special, even if we never accomplish a thing that would win us a trophy or medal.

There was an article in the local paper recently about a little Chihuahua who had only one eye, was arthritic and could hardly walk. In addition, this little fellow was fourteen years old, which is elderly for a small dog. But kids—and adults—love this little, crippled, half-blind dog because he accepts everybody as a friend. Children who are themselves deformed in some way feel as if he understands them, and they reach out to him and love him for being a role model for them. He is making a difference in this world, even though he would never win a medal in a dog show. He knows how to love.

So far we have talked about why we are afraid to die, but I think there is another aspect that we haven't touched on. That is because the process of dying is itself scary to us. So many illnesses have incredible pain associated with them, such as cancers, emphysema,

COPD, and others, and we fear how much we are going to have to suffer. I doubt that anyone would actively choose to be in horrible pain if they thought they could get away without it.

Let's be clear about one thing: Suffering and pain are not the same thing.

Pain is the physical sensation we get in our bodies when things are not working the way they should. This is not to say that it doesn't hurt; of course it does. No one is going to tell you otherwise. In fact, doctors and hospitals do their very best to control pain so that the body can heal as much as it is able to. In fact, pain is useful for calling our attention to whatever part hurts so that we can take some sort of action. But here's the thing: The resistance to pain makes it worse. If we can accept it as just a sensation and breathe into it, often it will lessen by itself.

When I was first in the hospital after my fall, I don't remember being in any pain at all, because the nurses gave me so much Percocet that I was out of it for the first few days. That was on purpose, so that my body wouldn't try to fight the pain and would allow as much healing as possible.

Suffering, on the other hand, is in the stories our minds tell us as to why we are sick, what we did wrong, and in the million and one thoughts that go through our heads when we have pain. "Is God punishing me for something I did or didn't do? Why me? Am I just cursed in some way? Oh, how am I going to take care of my kids when I'm sick? What will happen if I can no longer work?" And on and on.

Suffering, according to Roget's *Thesaurus*, may include such things as heartache, distress, sorrow, grief, or misery, none of which is the least bit pleasant, but it is not pain *per se*. Suffering does not *have* to accompany pain, but when it does, it so often has the element of resistance along with the physical discomfort.

I remember very clearly the summer I went back to my home town after my first year of teaching. The month of May for music teachers is a nonstop round of performances, especially for high school teachers. There are spring concerts, Baccalaureate and Graduation performances, grade cards that must be done, and closing up the room for the summer so that the custodial staff can varnish the floors, paint the walls, or do whatever else they need to do when the kids are gone.

So by the time I got home in June, I was a nervous wreck, and naturally I got sick. In fact, I had stomach cramps so bad that I passed out. My mom called the family doctor, who came to our house. (Doctors still did that in those days.) He gave me a shot of something or other that knocked me out for several hours.

But even before the doctor came, I remember feeling very peaceful. I was at home. I was being taken care of. All would be well. I knew it, and I was at peace. I even remember thinking, "Wow, here I am, hurting so badly, and it's okay. I am okay."

The point is I could have been blaming myself for not getting enough sleep, for working too hard, or for any number of things. But I did not. I was not suffering, even though I was in pain.

If we can just get our ego out of the way and quit thinking we have to *do something* to make ourselves feel better, often times the suffering will taper off, and we will just be left with the physical sensation of hurting. I am not trying to say here that suffering is a bad thing. Sometimes we just have to let ourselves feel how horrible everything is in order to let it go, and very often the simple act of surrendering to the pain will help it to dissipate.

I want to add just a short word here on the place of the ego, which so often gets the blame for whatever we feel is wrong in our lives. It seems as though the ego is an unwanted part of ourselves that we put up with even though it doesn't really do anything useful. That is unfair to the ego, I think. It serves us well by helping us know what our boundaries are with other people, for example, and by giving us a good sense our own Self. The ego wants to take care of us, and that is not all bad, but there is a time and a place for it to show up. If we can let it know—gently—that it doesn't have to fix everything for us, it can calm down.

Suffering is not something we have to experience unless we choose to. Again, we get to make that decision for ourselves. However, there are people who are especially susceptible to getting stuck in suffering. These are the Fours on the Enneagram, the sensitive souls who feel everything so deeply. Everything is high drama for them. If you understand that this is your particular way of relating to the world, it may help you to deal with whatever tragedy comes your way. The Four feels the beauty of things, as well, and it is that passion for life that helps Fours draw closer to the Divine. Thus Fours may experience higher highs and lower lows than other Types, but there are benefits to that way of relating to the Universe, as well.

I have a dear friend to whom everything is terrible, horrible, no-good, very bad, just like Alexander in the kids' book by Judith Viorst. Appropriately enough, the title of the book is *Alexander and the Terrible, Horrible, No-Good, Very Bad Day.* But fortunately for our friend, she is enlightened enough to be able to laugh at herself when she gets on one of her rants about how dire and gloomy her poor life is. She recognizes that she is a drama queen, even though she still falls into the trap every once in a while. The good part of her fixation is that it also allows her to see and enjoy the wonders that occur in her life.

We all play this game some of the time, but we don't have to keep ourselves stuck in the pattern unless we want to be there. We have the power to choose how we look at life.

If we are diagnosed with a terminal illness, though, then it may truly be pain we are dealing with. Cancer, especially in the late stages, can be extremely intense, but doctors and nurses are very good about trying to help people to control their hurting. The body just gets tired when trying to deal with it, and the medical folks know that. If this is your situation, by all means ask them for what you need.

It is when we are on the other side of the equation that things get difficult. What happens when someone we love dies? What makes one death seem like a terrible tragedy while another just feels like a natural ending?

Just recently some good friends of ours lost their daughter to a debilitating disease that wastes away the muscles and tissues while leaving the mind relatively intact. It is very difficult to watch someone die from this disease and know that there is nothing anyone can do to halt the inexorable downward spiral.

It was especially hard for our friends, because their daughter was quite young, and had a young family who had been quite close, both in proximity and emotionally. Laura's (name has been changed) son-in-law and the children had been taking care of her as best they could throughout the entire process. Laura herself had cut her work hours so that she could also be available to help out.

When Laura called me to tell me about Christine's death, I asked her how she was doing.

"Oh," she said, "I am tired a lot of the time. I can't go back to work full-time yet, because it's just too draining. Some days are okay, but at other times I feel like I am being pulled under by a giant wave. I wasn't prepared for the waves of grief that just wash over me sometimes. I thought I would be better by now."

And that's the thing with grief. It hits everyone differently. Some people seem to bounce back rather quickly, while for others grief seems to last forever. I have noticed that the age of the dying person and the circumstances surrounding the death make a difference as to whether a passing is a tragedy or an expected event in a long and well-lived life.

When my father died of a subarachnoid hemorrhage in 1974, he was a relatively young man who had never been sick a day in his life. So when he suddenly passed, I was devastated. It took me several years to come to terms with his dying, partly because up until the day before his death the doctors were optimistic that he would recover and be able to be moved to the Veterans' Hospital in Topeka for rehab. It was quite a shock when we got the news that he was gone.

Contrast that with my grandmother, who was 98 when she died. She had lived a full and good life, and while I was sorry that she was gone—I still miss her every day—I felt that she had done what she came here to do, with no regrets. She had been in a nursing home for nearly fifteen years, because she had trouble walking and needed help with everyday tasks. She was not really sick, just unable to care for herself. Today she would probably be in assisted living, but that wasn't an option at the time.

My mother visited her every day, and I don't think Grandma was too unhappy to be where she was, but she was tired of living when she died. Her body was just worn out. Death for her was a natural end to life, and she welcomed it with open arms.

On the other hand, when my childhood friend Andrew died in 2014, it hit me really hard. I had had no inkling that he was ill, and even his wife, Jody, thought he would be coming home from the hospital when he initially was admitted. Although he had had heart disease, this particular hospitalization didn't seem to be all that serious.

So the circumstances surrounding the death make a huge difference in the kind of grief we feel.

The renowned Swiss psychiatrist, Elisabeth Kubler-Ross (1926-2004), did a lot of work with dying patients during the 1960s, and in 1969 she published her ground-breaking work, *On Death and Dying*. As she was working with those who were very ill, she came up with the Five Stages of Grief. These stages apply both to the patient who is actively dying as well as to their loved ones who are watching them go through the process.

If you have been around someone you love, or have experienced a serious illness of your own, you may also have felt these same stages of trying to come to terms with what you are feeling.

The stages of grief are:

- Denial
- Anger
- Bargaining
- Depression
- Acceptance

In the first stage, Denial, the patient is overwhelmed with the diagnosis and doesn't believe it can possibly be happening to him or her. Thus he will often seek a second and even third opinion until he finally understands that, yes, he may only have six months to a year to live.

If the person has died from an accident or violent crime, you may expect to hear the survivors say, "But that can't be right! I was just talking to her on the phone a half hour ago!" Their minds have to learn a whole new reality, and it is a difficult transition to make.

Depending on the patient's age, Denial may be closely followed by Anger. "Why is this happening to me? What did I ever do to merit such a diagnosis? This isn't fair. I'm a good person!" might be some of the types of questions or comments a person may be making at such a time.

If we are the ones left behind by a loved one's unexpected or sudden death, there may also be anger that the one who died has left us alone and bereft. It just doesn't seem fair, even though the reaction of the survivor is entirely natural and may even be anticipated.

Sometimes people question why they or their loved one has received a fatal diagnosis, especially if they have been raised in a culture or belief system that tells them that illness is a punishment for sin. You may hear them say things like, "He's just too nice a person to have this happen to him." Or, "She is too young. He has young children at home. How will the family ever cope with her loss? What did he ever do to deserve such a punishment?"

In addition to the anger that people may feel, there may be a residual fear that it was somehow their fault or sin that caused their illness. Even as far back as Biblical times, people were asking Jesus, "Was it his sin or his parents' that this man was born blind?" (John 9: 1-12)

Jesus made it quite clear that sin didn't have anything to do with deformity or illness; it was just the way things were. No one was to blame.

However, this attitude can still be found in some countries where education is slow to take hold and people's attitudes may still reflect the thinking of thousands of years ago.

I remember reading an article about women in one of the African countries who developed cancer and as a consequence were then shunned by their families, as if there was something shameful about such a diagnosis. At the very time they most needed support from their loved ones, they were made to feel like pariahs.

I have a relative by marriage who is a well-educated woman. When she was diagnosed with breast cancer a few years ago, even she didn't want anyone in the family to know about it. It was if she felt that she was somehow "unclean" for having gotten a disease that unfortunately is too common among women these days. I had a very hard time understanding her attitude, because my own response to the same situation had been entirely different.

When I had cancer myself several years ago, I knew I needed to have as much support from my friends as possible. I told them all, and consequently was able to receive love and kindness when I most needed it.

I felt very bad for those African women who were left to deal with all the emotional upheaval as well as the difficulty of surgery, radiation and chemotherapy all alone, if indeed they had access to those therapies. How difficult that must be, and how alone they must feel.

Since the Anger stage rarely works to make the diagnosis go away, many people turn to Bargaining with God for a cure. "Just let me get well, and I promise I will be a better person. I will donate a third of my wealth to the poor; I will be nicer to my in-laws," and other such thoughts are attempts to make God listen to their pleas.

But Bargaining doesn't work very well, either. The sick person doesn't get well, and the one who tried to make a deal with God ends up feeling abandoned and let down because the prayers didn't make a difference. They may ultimately feel as though God doesn't care about them or their situation. Very likely, in this scenario, the next step is that the person becomes depressed. Nothing is working, and they are still sick. It is like they have been forsaken by God and by modern medicine.

Only after a period of Depression doesn't get them what they want, either, does the person finally get to Acceptance. "This is really going to happen; I am really going to die." Once that happens, often it is if a weight has been lifted from the person's spirit. Now they can get back to enjoying whatever time they have left.

Sometimes caregivers report that those who are in the final stages of life will suddenly start having dreams about beautiful gardens or big lush grassy areas where they see lots of people having fun and laughing. It would be tempting to think that dreams of this sort mean that the patient is on the road to recovery, but that thought would be wrong. In many cases, these types of dreams mean that the sick person has finally accepted that death is imminent, and is beginning to look forward to whatever comes next.

There was a young girl in my school whom I will call Amelia, which is not her real name, but that name fit her perfectly. For some reason, her parents usually dressed her in frilly white or pastel dresses, which gave her a somewhat otherworldly and old-fashioned look. I always felt that she would have been at home in Jane Austen's time, for there was something about her that didn't quite fit in the 20th century. Then too, her disease caused her body to age beyond her physical age, so she always looked a lot older than she really was.

When she finally realized toward the end of her life that death was imminent, she became almost luminous. Perhaps her intuitive understanding that she didn't have much time on this earth made her more in touch with the other side than the majority of children who never give death a thought.

The whole school turned out to celebrate her life on a beautiful day in May a couple of weeks before she died. There was a grand picnic on the school grounds, and she came dressed in her best lavender dress, while most of the other kids turned out in T-shirts and shorts. Some of her classmates had gathered around her, where she was sitting in her mom's lap, since she was too weak to get up and play with the other youngsters.

"Are you afraid to die?" they asked her.

"Oh, no," she replied, smiling. "I know I'm going to go to heaven. But," she continued slowly, "Jesus told me He's not done with me just yet."

There wasn't a dry eye in the crowd that heard her speaking so calmly and with such assurance. I am sure she brought a lot of peace to everyone present that day, along with the sadness that we were soon to lose such a beautiful, bright spirit. Even now, so many years later, I still get choked up remembering Amelia and what she taught us all.

Two weeks later, almost to the day, she died at home, once again sitting in her mother's lap, feeling her love until the very end. The teachers and her classmates and their parents all gathered again to celebrate her life in a church filled with purple balloons, which we released as we left. It was hard for most of us to see that small, white casket being slowly rolled out from the church to the waiting hearse. I can only imagine what her parents must have gone through that day, but I silently gave thanks to have known Amelia. What a graced gift this delightful child was.

When this acceptance finally happens for a dying person, it begins to be obvious that the sick one is beginning to disengage from the constraints of the egoic mind and resting in Spirit becomes very freeing, and there is no longer any need to accomplish anything. The time has come to allow whatever is coming to just be whatever it is. They can really experience the love of God in full, with no expectations, just the wondrous feeling of being totally loved. Amelia showed us all how to die gracefully.

Now the person can really begin to heal all the sorrows and wounds of a lifetime and to let go of all the petty problems and slights that previously seemed to be so huge. They just don't matter anymore. This is also the time to forgive family members or friends, to make amends or to give them your blessing. Dying can be a healing time for all those involved.

I remember when my friend Brianne, (not her real name), died a few years ago. All of the family had assembled in her hospital room to help her make her transition. Later her husband related to me that there was so much love in that space that the nurses remarked on how beautiful her passing was. Everyone who was there that night felt that they felt exquisitely blessed to have been a part of her death. It felt like a birth.

For my part, our mutual friend Celeste had called around nine o'clock to tell me that Brie was making her transition that night. I went to sleep feeling so much sadness that we were losing such a young, vibrant woman to cancer, but at the same time hoping that she would have a peaceful death.

It was around two o'clock in the morning when I had such a vivid dream that it woke me up. I had seen Brie in a gorgeous red velvet dress, and the two of us were out in the country somewhere, a lovely spot with a small stream running through it. Brie wanted to cross the brook using some rocks as stepping stones, but I hung back, afraid that I would fall into the rushing water. She leaped ahead joyously and easily, calling back over her shoulder to me.

"It's really easy when you know how!" she shouted. But I could not follow her. To this day I don't know if it was fear, or an instinctive knowing that it wasn't yet my time to go.

In fact, I didn't even realize just what the dream symbolized until the next morning, when Celeste phoned me around nine o'clock.

"Brie's gone," she said through her tears. "She died at about two this morning."

That's when I understood what my dream had meant.

You yourself may have had the experience of being around a dying person who almost seemed to glow or to be so radiant that it was hard to be sad in that moment. Death then becomes not a burden but a blessing. The one dying may see dead relatives or friends who come to welcome him or her Home with great joy. In their last few moments the person may have great care and concern for the younger members of the family, so that the whole experience is one of enormous love.

Steve Jobs' final words were said to be, "Wow! Oh, wow!" Crossing over must really be something special if Steve Jobs, the creator of the iPad and so many other remarkable devices had such a reaction to his own death.

Usually when someone has experienced such a passing they lose their fear of death. Some may realize that God is with them whether they are alive or dying, and that He will be there after death as well. My own belief is that there is no place we can be that God is not, and that includes the dying process.

When the phenomenon of having a near death experience first was reported in the 1980s it seemed almost like a fairy tale. Here were dozens of people telling about having passed through a long tunnel of light, only to meet their dead relatives and friends who were waiting for them on the other side. Sometimes Jesus, Moses, or some other religious figure would also be there as well. But regardless of who showed up to greet them, the experience seemed to be almost uniformly positive and uplifting. Almost all the people who had had such firsthand knowledge of what death was really like immediately lost their fear of dying. They understood that it was a transition to another state of being, and as such, wasn't remotely scary, only different from their existence on earth.

Anita Moorjani, an Indian woman who experienced an NDE during her bout with terminal cancer, detailed what it was like for her in her remarkable book, *Dying to Be Me*. The book became a bestseller, and she now travels the world giving talks and appearing on radio and television shows. The experience completely changed her life, and she is now healthy and able to help others to realize their own dreams.

Once a person has made that connection, as Anita Moorjani did, death can no longer be a fearsome thing; it is simply the next step on the journey. A lot of what seemed to be mysterious now seems to be perfectly natural. I would guess that it feels sort of like it does when we are ready to go on a long-awaited trip. We have made our plans, we've packed our bags, and now all that is left is to catch the shuttle to the airport. We may not know exactly what this trip will hold for us, but we are eager to get going and have this next exciting experience.

Then eternity becomes not some future that we cannot see, but a continuation of the life we already have within us. We may no longer have a physical body, but who we are in our core spirit probably is not really going to change all that much. It sounds to me like we have a lot to look forward to! Why would we fear to be as we are, only better? We won't have our egos to slow us down; we can just be joy, peace, and love. Sounds nice, doesn't it? It certainly sounds good to me.

While I am not in any hurry to leave this planet, the next step of the journey sounds like a grand adventure, something to be looked forward to as one would anticipate taking a trip to Europe or the Caribbean. Not scary at all, but still a mystery. I am looking forward to what the future holds!

CHAPTER 13

Conclusion

The subtitle of this book is *Seeking the Sacred in Everyday Life.* What does that mean, exactly? What things are sacred to us? Once we recognize that God, however we choose to see Him/ Her/ It/Them, is in charge of everything in the universe, then it becomes rather easy to acknowledge that all things belong in the category of sacred things. However, some things are easier to recognize as being sacred than others. We have talked about holy ground, for example, and what it means to be holy. But what about things that don't seem to fit into a nice, neat package called "holy?"

For instance, while it is fairly natural, comfortable, and even soothing to think of a gorgeous day in the mountains with family or friends as being sacred, other things such as the atrocities committed in times of war don't feel that way at all. If one has lost a child to a random shooting in the streets of one of our cities, it might be very hard indeed to see that as a sacred act.

I choose to think that God has a plan for all of humanity, and that the evolution of human behavior is part of that plan. What if all these seemingly unexplainable acts that seem so horrendous on one level serve as a way to elevate us to decide to live more lovingly, more in tune with our God-given nature as a result? That, of course, does not mean that we enjoy losing a precious child or loved one to random violence, nor does it mean that we must condone such behavior in others. But if we choose instead to see some sort of higher purpose at work, it gives our loss a monumentally more important meaning than just what appears at first glance.

In Germany during World War II, for example, six million Jews and other so-called "undesirables" such as disabled people, Gypsies, Catholics, and anyone else who disagreed with Hitler's government, were systematically exterminated in what was euphemistically called the Final Solution. The world was so shocked and appalled when word got out about the mass killings, that the motto became, "Never again."

I think something similar is happening right now with the Muslim people being in rather the same situation that affected so many Jews during the War. But there is one big difference. This time around, Jews and Muslims are working together to protect one another's businesses and places of worship. All around my city there are signs saying, "No matter where you come from or what you believe, you are welcome here." The signs have the same message in English, Arabic, and Spanish, because mass deportations of Mexican and Spanish-speaking people is also a very real possibility.

How can attitudes that attack others be sacred? The attitudes themselves are not, but if they can be used to teaching moments to help us elevate our ways of relating to one another in a higher form of love, then they indeed can be said to be raising the consciousness of humanity. Then our acts become a sacred response to difficult questions.

When we think about the sacredness of all things, that means that the smallest of God's creations, from the tiny ant crossing our sidewalk to the pesky fly buzzing against our open window is worthy to be called sacred. Each species has a part to play in the overall scheme of things, and when we lose one kind of animal or plant, it affects our whole world. Many people don't recognize this fact, though, and seem to think that some plants are nuisances or are just in the way of their way to make money. Thus, vast tracts of land are becoming devoid of the very trees, flowers, bushes, grasses, herbs, and vines that may be useful in curing cancers or other types of illness. Tigers, polar bears, and other species of animals, birds, fish and other sea creatures may disappear from the face of the earth unless we begin to realize that all of life is sacred, not just humans.

Our everyday life is full of the small sacred moments that we often take for granted. Seeing a baby smile or learn to walk for the first time, a six-year-old learning to ride her bicycle, the beauty of the gardens in our neighborhoods, the flowering crabapple and cherry trees in spring—all of these are sacred.

Sacred things are not just relegated to churches, synagogues, and mosques. They appear in the quiet times that an elderly couple spend together, just sitting on their front porch in their rocking chairs sipping their morning coffee and enjoying each other's company. The mother who lovingly prepares dinner for her family each night is performing a sacred act, as is the dad who coaches Little League or Pop Warner with his kids. The hospice nurse who is a constant presence helping a family prepare to lose a loved one is as holy as any priest, rabbi, or imam.

The very air we breathe is full of God's presence. Our heartbeat pulses with His love for us. Our bodies are marvelous creations that always will strive to stay alive, until they are finally overcome and succumb to death. Even death is sacred, for it means we are about to return Home from whence we came.

The only reason we don't recognize all these things as holy is that we are not aware of them. Once we begin to see our life as holy, all manner of things show up for us to look at and consider sacred. Keeping a journal in which we write down a few things each day for which we are grateful is a wonderful way to expand our appreciation for the sacred things in our own lives. I sometimes make it a game in which I don't allow myself to repeat something I've said before. So if on Monday I have written that I'm thankful for the great weather we've had this week, then I can't repeat that as one of the things I see as sacred. Sometimes I get to the point when I say, "I'm grateful that nothing hurts today." Or, "The electricity is working today." Usually it *is* working, but if I haven't yet said I'm thankful for it, into the journal it goes.

In other words, everything in our life is something that demonstrates Grace at work in our lives. We all have so much to be thankful for, even if there are days when we just feel out of sorts and mad at the world. Even those days have a sacred purpose. Perhaps it is to tell us that something we are longing for and hoping will happen will come, just not now. The time is not yet right for the longed-for event to occur. That's not to say that it will not happen; it will come in its own time. Or if that thing is not right for us, is somehow not on purpose for our life's sacred plan, then the thing that *is* right will show up instead. If we can keep an open mind and are willing to let the "right thing" happen, we don't have to worry about the how of it all. Let God handle the details.

Our very life is sacred, so what we experience will also be sacred, if we choose to view it in that light. God is in charge here, not me, and not you. He/She will orchestrate the events perfectly to help us learn what we came here to discover. Then when we look back over a period of years and see what has actually occurred we are amazed at how exquisitely our life has turned out.

The sacred is in everything we do, see, or have in our lives. Every once in a while, we need to stand still and give thanks for what we have. Life is good!

PART TWO

Resources for Entering the Stillness

Resources for Entering the Stillness

This section is different from Part One, in that I have chosen to include here a group of meditations and prayers that I have found to be helpful throughout the years. It is not intended to be a comprehensive list, and not every spiritual practice will appeal to everyone. They are not intended to. Some things I have included simply for information; others are actual practices that can be done by anyone.

I have also included authors whose work I find inspirational or thought-provoking, as well as music that is nice for meditation. Most of the books are available in bookstores or on Amazon. You may already have a collection of these things, and it really doesn't matter what the particular selection is as long as it is of value to you.

In general, if you are intending to start a meditation practice, there are a few things to know before beginning. You need not have a special area in your home set aside for contemplation, but I think it is helpful to do so, just because that area then becomes your own sacred space. You can have a small altar there if you so choose, but it is not necessary. Over time, the place you choose to be your reflection space becomes your holy place whether or not you have candles, icons, or other items that are special to you.

In the same way, it is not necessary to wear special garments, although some people like to have a hooded sweater or shawl, since it may become chilly when one sits for an extended period of time. In addition, a special piece of clothing sends a signal to your body that you are now ready to enter a role different from your regular routine. A priest robing for Mass has a similar intention.

Usually twenty to thirty minutes is about the right amount of time. Longer than that and you may go to sleep; less time may not give your body the opportunity to enter the deep relaxation that you need to experience the maximum benefit.

Before you start your session, be sure to take care of any business that needs attention so that your body is ready to enter the stillness. You don't want to have to go to the bathroom or answer the telephone while you are in this period of relaxation. If it is your intention to spend this time as a way to encounter the Holy One, or even if you just intend to make it a period for relaxation, you need to be able to be present without worry or distraction.

There are various ways to sit while entering the stillness. Some people prefer the lotus position while seated on the floor, but if you have bad knees, this may not be possible for you, since the lotus position is cross-legged with your feet on top of the opposite leg. It is perfectly all right to sit in a chair with your feet on the floor. To some extent your choice of posture will depend upon your health and physical condition, but it is entirely your choice. Some people prefer to be barefoot or in stocking feet, but again it really doesn't matter. It is totally a matter of preference.

One thing to be aware of is that deep meditation, especially if it is done for many months or years, may start to bring up psychological issues that need to be dealt with. Sometimes you may need to forgive another person or yourself, or you may need to let go of old patterns, vows, or beliefs, some of which you may not be aware of until they suddenly show up. If at any time the material seems to be more than you can handle by yourself, by all means consult a reputable therapist to help you. Sometimes a neutral person can help you deal with things more easily than you can do by yourself. Such a person can become a trusted ally.

Definitely see a therapist if you should become depressed or feel suicidal. That is a sign to stop meditating and see a mental health professional. Get help before going on; otherwise you may make things worse.

I have also included specialized vocabulary in this section that may be new to some people. Formal types of prayers are also included here, as are some of my favorite teachers and authors.

Aura

The aura is the energetic body that is outside of the physical body. It may extend about three feet in all directions in a sort of bubble around us. If we are energized and excited, our energy becomes very fast; in such cases the aura may extend much farther than three feet. If you practice expanding your awareness, you may be able to feel your aura growing. Likewise, when we are feeling down, or sad, or depressed, our aura may shrink to become much closer to our physical bodies.

Benson, Dr. Herbert (1935-)

Dr. Benson is the author of *The Relaxation Response,* which was one of the first works to deal specifically with sitting quietly for a given period of time to help deal with the effects of stress on the body. He coined the term to give a scientific name to the process of meditation. Dr. Benson is a cardiologist who founded the Mind/Body Institute at Massachusetts General Hospital in Boston and is a professor of mind/body medicine at Harvard Medical School. He has written extensively on the subject, both in scientific articles and books.

Bindi

The bindi is the small red dot Indian women wear in the center of their foreheads. It is used to represent wisdom and wholeness and is placed in the spot for the Sixth Chakra, also known as the Third Eye.

Dr. Borysenko, Joan

Dr. Joan Borysenko is a well-known author who has a Ph.D. in Medical Sciences from Harvard, and she trained in three post-doctoral areas, cancer cell biology, behavioral medicine, and psychoneuroimmunology. She studied with Dr. Herbert Benson, and with him was a co-founder of a Mind/Body clinic. In 1987 she published *Minding the Body, Mending the Mind*, which became a best-seller. She now travels and lectures while continuing to write books on many topics, including *It's Not the End of the World,* which is about how to become more resilient when we are faced with life's problems.

Chakras

According to Hindu tradition, there are seven major chakras, or energy centers, which run up the spinal column of the human body. They may be imagined as looking like colored wheels that speed up or slow down according to our emotional and physical states. There are also chakras in the palms of the hands, the soles of the feet, and above the head. The chakras of the feet allow our energy to reach deep into the earth, almost like roots to ground us.

If we receive massages, the therapist may gently stroke the soles of our feet before starting the actual work in order to allow us to enter a state of relaxation. When the massage is finished, she or he may press her thumbs into the center of the bottoms of the feet to encourage a return to full wakefulness. With a little practice, we can become aware of the energy of the feet even without massage.

The same thing is true for the palms of the hands. If we rub our hands together vigorously for a few seconds and then hold the hands about three or four inches apart, we can often feel the energy flowing between the hands. That is why some paintings and figures of Jesus, Mary, and the saints show them with the palms of the hands facing out; they are sending healing energy to the world in this posture. I have a small statue of Mary that is called Our Lady of Grace, which shows her in exactly this pose. I would assume then that what we Christians call Grace is similar to what the Hindus call energy. At the very least, they seem to have many of the same kind of qualities.

The Base Chakra, the lowest of the seven that align along the spine, is located at its base, where the "sitting bones" are; it is also referred to as the "grounding chakra." It serves to anchor us to the earth and to our family, our tribe. The tribe can take the form of a large family group, a nation, or loyalty to our religion or even our college or favorite sports team. It helps to give us our identity and to know where we belong on the earth. Because of its early association with the tribe, it has a lot to do with survival issues, since without them in ancient times we would not have been able to live for long. We needed each other for food, shelter, and to protect the group from enemies. The color for this energy is red.

The Second Chakra is orange, and it is the seat of our creativity and our sexuality. It is found in the genital area. It is the energy that allows us to move away from our family of origin to found our own family with spouse and children of our own. In this way it is still anchored to family, but it is wider in scope than the original focus in the First Chakra.

The Third Chakra is in the area of the belly. It is ruled by the will, and it is also where we learn to trust our instincts about others and the situations in which we find ourselves. When we say we "trust our gut," this is the chakra we mean. Its color is yellow, so when we say that someone is "yellow-bellied" we mean that the person doesn't trust his own instincts and so is a coward.

The Fourth Chakra is in the heart area and is where we find love and compassion for others. As we progress up the spinal area, the frequency at which the chakras vibrate grows faster. The first three chakras may be seen as wheels vibrating with energy from the earth; the Fourth through Seventh chakras begin to let the divine force in as well. These energies allow us to step outside of ourselves to care for others who are not part of our original family, tribe, religion, or nation. The color here is green, the color of new life.

The Fifth Chakra is blue and governs the throat area. It represents how we present ourselves to the world through our speech and the other ways we communicate. This level is less about identifying with a special group and more about reaching out to others outside of our immediate clan as a teacher or other type of communicator, such as a TV anchor or motivational speaker. It is about speaking our truth to the world, so that someone described as being "true blue" is seen as a person who is honest and trustworthy.

The Sixth Chakra is also sometimes called the Third Eye and is located between the eyes and slightly above them in the center of the forehead. It represents wisdom, knowledge, and understanding. It is the area where new insights come from. In India, married women wear the *bindi,* a small red dot, in this very spiritual spot which is close to the Crown Chakra. Its color is indigo.

The Seventh or Crown Chakra is sometimes represented as a lotus blossom with many petals. It may be pink, gold, white, or even violet in color, and it is the center where divine energy is the strongest. It is why saints and angels are often painted with haloes, a recognition by Christian artists of the reality of the energy that is present there, even though they may never have heard of the chakra system. I have even seen paintings that show that energy as a flame emanating from the crown of the head, which always makes me think of Pentecost, since that feast recognizes the occasion on which the Holy Spirit appeared for the first time to the Apostles. The Gospel writers were more attuned to the energetic world than they knew!

Chakra Cleanse/Energy Manipulation

Here is a simple little exercise to use when you are feeling overwhelmed or stressed out.

Close your eyes as you would for any other meditation, and take a few cleansing breaths to center yourself. Then imagine the energy that is all around your body, extending about three feet in all directions. Slowly breathe that energy up through your spinal column and let it pour out from your crown chakra and down the whole body. Do this three times, allowing the energy to sink easily back into the earth as you finish the set.

Next, direct the energy up the left side of your body and over the top of your head, imagining it is flushing out any negativity or impurities down your right side. Again, do this part three times, letting the old energy return to the earth easily and naturally.

Now repeat this process, this time bringing the energy up the front of your body, over the top of your head, and flushing out any old negative patterns, vows, or beliefs down your back. Again, do the exercise three times.

Repeat the procedure starting at the bottom of the right side of your body, over the top of your head and down the left side, doing the whole thing three times as before.

The next time, imagine the energy moving up your back, over the top, and down the front of your body to release any stuck places or tight, tense muscles. You can again release energy that has been in your cells because of old patterning, vows, or beliefs, doing the exercise three times as usual.

These first four times are for getting rid of what no longer serves you; the final step is to re-energize your whole body from the inside out. Take a deep breath to bring up clean, pure energy from all around yourself and let it pour down inside, coming through your crown chakra. This last sequence may take longer than the others, and you may take many more than three breaths, because you will be directing this new energy inside to fill up all of your cells, your bones, muscles, tendons, nerves—all of you. You may imagine this energy to be white light, or you may see it as iridescent, pink, gold, or any other color you like. If you do this exercise often, you may find that some days your body will love the green of new life, or the swirly purple, orange, and red of vibrant health. Be sure to take as long as you need so that you can get the full benefit of this glowing, resplendent, new you, alive with wellbeing and vitality.

Chopra, Deepak, M.D. (1947-)

Dr. Chopra is a world-renowned physician who now runs a wellness clinic in California and teaches the Ayurveda method of healthy eating. In addition, he is a prolific writer; many of his books are about spirituality and healing. Some of his titles are *The Seven Spiritual Laws of Success, Quantum Healing*, and *Ageless Body, Timeless Mind.* He has a rather unique perspective on things, since he was born in India into the Hindu culture but also has a good understanding of Christianity. He lectures frequently around the U.S.

Dyer, Wayne W. (1940-2015)

The late Wayne Dyer wrote many wonderful and inspirational books about self-help and the spiritual life. His books include *Your Erroneous Zones, Manifest Your Destiny, The Power of Intention,* and *Inspiration.* I find these books very helpful, and I return to them again and again. He is one of my favorite authors.

The Enneagram

The Enneagram (ENNY-a-gram) is an ancient method of classifying human behavior into nine distinct Types. ("Ennea" means nine in Greek.) It has become popular in recent years due to the work of Armenian mystic, philosopher, and spiritual teacher Georges Ivanovich Gurdjieff. Two good modern sources of information about the system are Don Richard Riso and Ross Hudson, who are widely credited with being the authorities on the subject. However, Richard Rohr and Andreas Ebert have also written a book which considers the material from a Catholic standpoint. Studying the Types and learning which group we identify with helps us to understand why we do the things we do, and why it is so hard to break patterns that have been with us all of our lives.

As long as we don't fall into the trap of trying to identify and classify all our friends and relations, tempting though that may be, the Enneagram is an invaluable tool for self-knowledge. We must remember that the Type we present to the world is simply our persona, or mask, and not who we really are.

The Types fall into three sub-categories, which can be thought of as Body Types (Eight, Nine, and, and One), Emotional Types (Two, Three, and Four), and Mind Types (Five, Six, and Seven). While all of us at one time or another act from each of the Types, we usually identify primarily with one of them. I am presenting them here starting with the Body Types as a group, which begin with Eight rather than One.

Body Types, also known as Instinctive Types

- Type Eight: The Challenger. This Type can be very powerful and dominating, but they also are wonderful protectors of the family, which is why they often appear as policemen or are in the Armed Forces. Their big fear is to be controlled or harmed by another; thus they seek to protect themselves and others from danger. They are often dynamic and energetic, forthright in their manner, and they make good leaders.
- Type Nine: The Peacemaker. This Type is often seen as being easygoing, while inside they fear loss and separation from loved ones. Their biggest desire is for peace, and they are frequently spiritual seekers as well as mediators of conflicts since they become uneasy with discord, either within themselves or with others. Even though they are so attuned to the inner world of the spirit, they are also very grounded in their own bodies. They are usually very patient and accepting of others.
- Type One: The Reformer. This person wants to do things just because they are the right thing to do. They really want to be seen as being good and virtuous, and they uphold the law and follow the rules. They fear being seen as bad, or wrong, or defective in some way, and they hold themselves and others to high standards of conduct. They make good teachers, but they must take care not to insist on perfection. They are very ethical and reliable, fair and honest in their dealings with others.

Emotional Types

- Type Two: The Helper. This person is seen as being caring and generous to a fault. They fear being unloved and not being wanted for themselves, but they truly want to help others. Their families and close friends are very dear to them, and people often gravitate to their kindness. They must be careful to take care of themselves as well as they do others; otherwise their health may suffer. They are empathetic and giving, and are usually compassionate and focused on other people.

- Type Three: The Achiever. Threes are driven to be successful, because their biggest fear is that they are worthless without their achievements, their beauty, or their money and position. They really want to feel that others like them for who they are, not just for what they have accomplished. But they are the ones who do extraordinary things: They become CEOs, they excel in the entertainment world and in politics. They are true leaders, often very creative and attractive.
- Type Four: The Individualist. Fours can be great artists, for they admire beauty and often have a quirky sense of style in their manner and dress. They want to be seen as special in some way, and they are extremely creative in whatever field they enter. They fear being unnoticed and that they might be perceived as being nobody special, so they create their lives in such a way as to draw attention to themselves. They make excellent writers and designers of clothing or home decoration. They are imaginative and sensitive and sometimes feel very vulnerable. They have tender hearts.

Mind Types

- Type Five: The Investigator. The ones who identify as Fives love information, and they want to learn as much as they can. They are often innovators in the sciences or specialists in a particular subject they have studied intensely. They are fearful that they will not be able to handle things or will be helpless, so they study a lot to make sure they can care for themselves. Fives often relate better to books, ideas, and things than they do with people, but they are the ones who create the latest and greatest technological designs for iPhones and other useful devices. They want to be seen as being capable and competent at whatever they do. They are often the experts in their fields that others turn to. They are thoughtful and perceptive and may have insights that others miss.

- Type Six: The Loyalist. Sixes are often consumed with worry and anxiety, because their basic fear is of not being supported by others or being unable to survive by themselves. They look for security and safety, which makes them ideal people to design products that won't fail when the consumer gets them home. They are loyal friends and romantic partners, and they are extremely trustworthy and responsible. They are the dependable ones others seek out in a crisis.
- Type Seven: The Enthusiast. This Type wants to experience it all. They love fun and adventure, and their calendars are always full so that they don't miss out on anything. Their biggest fear is to be deprived, so they seek fulfillment in doing interesting and sometimes dangerous things, such as hang-gliding or climbing mountains without technical support. On the other hand, because they like trying new things, they can be very productive and innovative. They have quick and enthusiastic minds, and they are able to see applications that others might miss. They are a lot of fun to be around.

Obviously, I have given only a brief summary of each Type; there is much more about each of them than I can include here. For instance, there are Wings on either side of a person's main Type. For me as a Nine, I have Wings of Eight and One, which means I also have some of the characteristics of those Types as well as my own Nine qualities. This is true for all Types.

Guided Meditations

Guided meditation is one good way to get into the stillness. This type of meditating is different from Centering Prayer and Transcendental Meditation in that the one doing the meditating is guided by another person who is reading from a prepared script. These scenarios may be fanciful, and we enter them via a staircase or elevator that we imagine however we choose to see them. We may or may not have a mentor, a person or figure such as an angel, a dead relative, or some other wise and helpful person who will be our helper throughout the process. This person ideally is someone we trust to have our best interests at heart, so that we feel safe and secure at all times. For children, sometimes this figure might be Superman or Pooh Bear, for example.

When we arrive at our destination, which may be the ocean, a beautiful forest, or some other special and meaningful place, the reader will guide us through the exercise. The location may be real or imaginary. Sometimes there is a particular emphasis on a special problem, such as preparing for surgery or healing from an illness. Usually we will feel relaxed and energized when we finish such an exercise.

Many people have recorded this type of guided meditation. Joan Borysenko, Pat Kendall, and Brian Weiss are a few.

I have created an exercise that is based on Ps. 47, the famous saying, "Be still and know that I AM God" as an example of one type of guided meditation. This style of meditating could also be used with other Scripture or sacred readings, sort of like *Lectio Divina*, in which one focuses upon one particular word at a time. I have done this type of focused falling into the sacred space with the Psalms, for example, but the process is the same in any case.

Begin as you would with any meditation, taking a few calming breaths and letting your mind and body relax. Then speak the entire line to yourself, as you would in *Lectio Divina*. You may find thoughts arising, or not. Keep repeating the phrase, with special attention to the word God. You may find you are substituting other names for God: Sat-Chit-Ananda, All That Is, Yahweh, Allah, Source, the Living Light. Or perhaps you are attracted to the very being-ness of the Eternal One. Whatever comes up for you is all right.

Eventually your mind will come to stillness with that part of the phrase and will begin to move on to the next. You may use the I AM of the Old Testament as a whole, because that is how God called Himself when Moses asked His name, or you may go to the "am" part alone. Either one is fine. This is your meditation.

Now you are at the word "that." You may find yourself repeating as the Buddhists do, "This is That, and That is That," which acknowledges the unity of all things, or you may come up with something entirely different. Whatever you settle on is fine, and you may find you are hearing or seeing in your mind's eye something else completely.

When you have finished with as much as you need for now, go to the word "know." How many ways are there of knowing? What is your favorite way to know things? Or does it depend on the thing you are learning? Again, do this part as long as it feels right to you.

What does "and" mean to you? And what? And what else? Keep going until you run out of steam, then move on to the next word.

"Still." Use the same process as before.

"Be." By this time in the proceedings you should be feeling completely relaxed and still. Continue until you feel finished.

I have found that this exercise sometimes takes more than twenty minutes, so leave a little extra time. Or you may find yourself being drawn to meditating on only one or two words in the whole phrase, and that is all right, too. Different things will arise on different days, so allow yourself to be surprised!

Home Altar

Since I dealt with this topic earlier in the book, I won't belabor the point here, except to say that you may make this as elaborate as you wish, but it is not necessary to create a special place for meditation. All I have where I meditate is a shawl, a stone that reminds me that God is strong and sure, and a comfortable chair that makes it restful to sit for twenty minutes. I also have a watch with easy-to-read numbers so that I can keep track of the time. There is also an app that you can download to your phone that plays the "Veni Sancte Spiritus" and is timed for twenty minutes. A Centering Prayer group that I sometimes attend uses this app, which frees the mind from having to wonder how long we have been meditating.

Journaling

Journaling is a wonderful way to access deep-seated problems and discover one's inner self. Since I wrote about this topic at length, see Chapter 11 for more information.

Keating, Thomas, O.C.S.O. (1923-)

Father Thomas Keating is a Trappist monk who resides at St. Benedict's Abbey in Snowmass, Colorado. He is one of three priests who developed the method of contemplation called Centering Prayer, which is based on the 14th Century work, *The*

Cloud of Unknowing. This book, written by an anonymous monk who apparently wanted to teach the young men in his monastery how to meditate, is one of the spiritual classics. Along with his fellow priests at the Abbey, Father William Meninger and Father Basil Pennington, Father Keating started Contemplative Outreach, a program which encourages lay people to meditate. It also provides educational and spiritual support for smaller local groups. Once a year Contemplative Outreach holds a national conference at which noted contemporary writers such as Ilia Delio, O.S.F., Richard Rohr, and Cynthia Borgeault are the featured presenters.

Some of Father Thomas's books are *Open Mind, Open Heart: The Contemplative Dimension of the Gospel and Invitation to Love: The Way of Christian Contem-plation.*

Labyrinth

A labyrinth is an ancient system of walking meditation, the form of which takes the walker first toward, then away from the center four times before reaching the open space in the middle of the circle which represents the soul, God, or the Higher Self. The labyrinth is designed to foster contemplation while slowly walking the path. Sometimes Christian labyrinths, if viewed from above, can be seen to have the form of the four arms of a cross inside the winding circular path.

The most famous labyrinth is the one built inside the Cathedral in Chartres, France, at some time between 1124 and 1220 C.E., but many other denominations, including Tibetan Buddhism, use labyrinths as well. St. Paul's Episcopal Church in Fort Collins, Colorado, has a labyrinth on the west side of the church proper that is set into a garden with lovely landscaping, providing a serene space for reflection. This photo shows the post at the entrance to the labyrinth.

Lectio Divina

Lectio Divina, or Divine Reading, was another early Christian way of praying that fell out of favor and has recently been revived. It was first started by Origen in the third century as a way for Christians to remember Jesus and to focus on His life. It was usually done in a group so as to foster community, especially during the heyday of the monasteries.

Nowadays Lectio usually focuses on a part of a Gospel reading or St. Paul's letters to the early Christian communities. Often practitioners of Lectio choose to use one of the Psalms or another reading from the Old Testament, or sometimes contemporary spiritual writers such as Sister Macrina Wiederkehr, O.S.B. of St. Scholastica's

Monastery of Fort Smith, Arkansas. Sister Macrina is a very wise woman who writes a blog, "A Few Things I Want to Say Before I Die." Some of her books are *A Tree Full of Angels, Abide*, and *Seasons of Your Heart.*

Lectio has a four-part form to be followed. The object is not to learn something from the chosen reading, but instead to allow the passage to seep into your bones.

The first step is to choose a passage that you like. It may be one or two sentences, but not more than that, because you want to be able to remember the whole thing. Read it several times, slowly and reverently, aloud if possible. As that is taking place, you will soon notice that one word or another pops out at you as being especially important. At that point, stop reading and just let the word resonate within you. Now you are entering the second step, letting the words seep into your bones.

For example, suppose you are reading the passage in Matt.5:3 that is "Blessed are the poor in spirit, for theirs is the kingdom of heaven." (NIV)

Any one of those words may present itself on a given day. Perhaps what sticks out for you this time is "the poor in spirit." Who exactly are the poor in spirit? What is it that makes them "poor?" This is the meditation part of the Lectio reading, so don't be in too much of hurry to leave this sacred time. You don't have to follow my questions; see what comes up for you. It may be very different than what I am suggesting.

Part 3 is called Prayer, which is speaking to God and then listening to His answer. Perhaps you understand the part about being poor as referring not to being poor in the sense of not having any money, but rather about letting go of your own sense of importance. You don't care if anyone thinks you are spiritual or not.

The last part of Lectio is contemplation. In this section, you just allow the words to become part of your experience rather than focusing expressly on them as we did earlier in the process. In this section, you may feel warmth, or perhaps the sensation of someone laying his hands on you in blessing or as an anointing. In any case, it probably will feel good and have a quality of comfort about it.

An optional last step would be to copy the reading down onto a small card that you can carry around with you, or to write in your journal.

Lectio is sometimes done as a group exercise rather than a solo effort; each way has benefits and drawbacks. It is more private when done alone, of course, but once in a while it is nice to have the feedback of others in the group, because different words will have presented themselves to each person. That can lead to lively discussion and a broader understanding of the material than is possible if you are by yourself.

In any case, Lectio is a good tool for prayerful meditation.

One can also use music as a way to do Lectio. You can even do this lying down (with headphones, so as not to disturb your partner if you have one. It is not advisable to do this while driving, however, since your attention at that time needs to be on the road and not on meditation. If the music is instrumental, you can just choose a song or playlist that allows you to relax while you are listening. If, however, the music has words, it is probably better to choose something sacred that speaks to you. I love the Psalms, because there are so many of them (150) and there is something for nearly every emotional state. Catholic composers such as Bob Hurd, Marty Haugen, David Haas, John Michael Talbot, Daniel Schutte, and others have wonderful music that lends itself to this type of meditating.

If you know the music well, you may choose to sing it inside your own head and use it as you would any other phrase as explained for Lectio Divina above. I find this is a very useful way to meditate, especially if I am upset about something. A song that tells me not to be afraid because God is always near helps a lot.

Meditation

Meditation is any method of sitting still or being quiet, or eyes-open walking that focuses the mind, either on the breath alone or on a given subject. Sometimes a mantra or sacred word is used for this purpose, but it is not a requirement.

Since this whole book is about meditating, either for spiritual purposes or for relaxation, I will not go into detail here, except to say that one either is trying to empty the mind, as in Centering Prayer, or to focus it, as in guided meditations.

Meninger, William, O.C.S.O.

Father William Meninger is one of the Trappist priests, along with Father Thomas Keating and Father Basil Pennington, who popularized the use of Centering Prayer in the 1970s. Father William is also an author who has written several spiritual books, and he regularly teaches workshops on the Enneagram, Teresa of Avila, St. John of the Cross, as well as those on Centering Prayer.

Pennington, Basil, O.C.S.O.

Father Basil Pennington is the third member of the group from St. Benedict's Abbey at Snowmass, Colorado, who popularized Centering Prayer during the 1970s. He is also an author of several books on spiritual topics.

The Rosary

The Rosary is a Catholic form of prayer that recalls Jesus's life. It is a type of guided meditation, in that the pray-er directs his or her attention to specific events in the lives of Jesus and Mary instead of trying to empty the mind. Different days of the week focus on the various episodes recounted in the Bible. For example, Mondays and Thursdays are the Joyful Mysteries, which relate the stories about Jesus's early life up to age twelve; Tuesdays and Fridays are the Sorrowful Mysteries that tell of His Passion and Death; Wednesdays, Saturdays, and Sundays follow the Glorious Mysteries, which tell of His Resurrection, Ascension, Pentecost, Mary's Assumption, and her crowning as the Queen of Heaven.

In recent years another category has been added, which is called the Luminous Mysteries. These five events tell of Jesus's baptism in the Jordan River, the first miracle at the wedding in Cana of Galilee, the proclamation of the kingdom of heaven, the Transfiguration, and the Last Supper.

A rosary has the beads divided into sets of ten. In between is a single bead on which the pray-er says one Our Father, one Hail Mary, and one Glory Be to the Father. The other ten are Hail Marys with a Glory Be at the end of each set. The creed is said on the crucifix, plus a single Our Father, three Hail Marys, and one Glory Be.

Rose Window

A rose window is a common type of round stained glass design used in Catholic and other Christian churches. It may be placed above the altar or over the entrance door so that parishioners see it on the way out of the church. It may show Jesus, Mary, the Holy Spirit in the form of a dove, or rays radiating out from a sun that represents the love of God. Rose windows are usually in the shape of a mandala, with equal divisions in the area surrounding the main image. They may also show the bread and wine, or more generic symbols, such as roses or other flowers, or sheaves of wheat and bunches of grapes.

Sacred Music

I mentioned earlier in the Lectio Divina section that sacred music can be a powerful tool in helping achieve relaxation as well as aiding in the search for holiness in one's life. Under that subtitle I talked about mostly Catholic music, but other traditions have many good things to offer as well.

I especially like the Sanskrit chants of Deva Premal and Miten, who have recorded several albums of sacred Hindu music. They are really wonderful done in a group setting, and they repeat often enough that even if you don't speak Sanskrit you can usually pick them up fairly easily. You can also enjoy them by yourself; just don't listen to them in the car or in bed, as they have long periods of silence punctuated by a Tibetan singing bowl or bell, and that can startle you if you are somewhere else in your mind.

Some of the Native American music is also delightful, and R. Carlos Nakai and Peter Kater have some exquisite music recorded. Joanne Shenandoah and Alice Gomez are other good choices for this kind of meditation. Some of the Celtic recordings would be suitable, as are the Tibetan monks chanting. Many of the Solitude albums also would work well.

Since we're on the topic of monks chanting, some of the Catholic monasteries, both men and women, have nice ethereal music that can transport you to another dimension. Hildegard of Bingen's music is exceptionally nice, and there are settings by groups called Sequentia and Anonymous 4.

Taize albums are also good, either for group settings or if you are alone. The Taize movement began in France, and they have recorded sacred Catholic music with easy refrains that everyone can sing, while the verses are then sung in many different languages. It is an attempt to make the music truly ecumenical and universal.

Stations of the Cross

The Stations are a form of walking meditation which can be done alone or with a group. Most Catholic and Episcopal churches have the representations of the Stations on the walls around the interior of the worship space. These may be done as paintings or statues, simple or elaborate. They are there to assist the worshiper to follow Jesus's steps as He walked from the Temple in Jerusalem to Mount Calvary where He was crucified. If one is praying alone, he or she walks the Stations in silence, respectfully entering into the last few hours of Jesus's life meditatively. If they are said congregationally, the parishioners stay in the pews, and only the priest walks the Stations, leading the congregation in the meditations at each one.

Fourth Station: Jesus Meets His Sorrowful Mother

St. Elizabeth Ann Seton Catholic Church, Fort Collins, Colorado

BIBLIOGRAPHY

Acevedo Butcher, Carmen. *Man of Blessing: A Life of St. Benedict.* Paraclete Press, Brewster Massachusetts, 2006.

Acevedo Butcher, Carmen. St. Hildegard of Bingen: Doctor of the Church. Paraclete Press, Brewster, Massachusetts, 2007, 2013.

Anonymous. *The Cloud of Unknowing* and *The Book of Privy Counsel.* Newly edited, with an Introduction by William Johnston. Image Books, a Division of Doubleday & Company, Inc. 1973.

Bays, Brandon. *Freedom Is: Liberating Your Boundless Potential.* New World Library, Novato, California. 2006.

Bays, Brandon. *The Journey: A Practical Guide to Healing Your Life and Setting Yourself Free.* Atria Paperback. New York, London, Sydney, Toronto, New Delhi. 1999, 2012.

Bays, Brandon. *Living the Journey: Using The Journey Method to Heal Your Life and Set Yourself Free.* Edited by Patricia Kendall, Ph.D. and Lesley Strutt, Ph.D.Atria Paperback. New York, London, Sydney, Toronto, New Delhi. 2012.

Beil, Maria-Thomas, O.S.B., Abbess Emerita. *St. Walburga and Her Impact Through the Centuries: A Woman of Faith, Courage and Love.* The Abbey of St. Walburga, Virginia Dale, Colorado, 2014.

Borysenko, Joan, Ph.D. *Fire in the Soul: A New Psychology of Spiritual Optimism.* Warner Books, New York, 1993.

Borysenko, Joan, Ph.D. *Guilt Is the Teacher, Love Is the Lesson: A Book to Heal You, Heart and Soul.* Warner Books, New York City, 1990.

Borysenko, Joan, Ph.D. *Inner Peace for Busy People: 52 Strategies for Transforming Your Life.* Hay House, Inc. Carlsbad, California, Sydney, Australia. 2001.

Borysenko, Joan, Ph.D. *Minding the Body, Mending the Mind.* Simon and Schuster Sound Ideas. (audiotape with relaxation sequences) 1988.

Borysenko, Joan, Ph.D. and Miroslav Borysenko. *The Power of the Mind to Heal: Renewing Body, Mind, and Spirit.* Hay House, Inc., Carlsbad, California, 1994.

Dyer, Dr. Wayne W. *Change Your Thoughts, Change Your Life: Living the Wisdom of the Tao.* Hay House, Inc., Carlsbad, California; London, Sydney, Johannesburg, Vancouver, Hong Kong, New Delhi. 2007.

Dyer, Dr. Wayne W. *Inspiration: Your Ultimate Calling.* Hay House, Inc., Carlsbad, California; London, Sydney, Johannesburg, Vancouver, Hong Kong. 2006.

Dyer, Dr. Wayne W. *The Power of Intention: Learning to Co-create Your World Your Way.* Hay House, Inc., Carlsbad, California; London, Sydney, Johannesburg, Vancouver, Hong Kong. 2004.

Dyer, Dr. Wayne W. *There's a Spiritual Solution to Every Problem.* Quill, an Imprint of HarperCollins Publishers. 2001.

Dyer, Dr. Wayne W. *Your Sacred Self: Making the Decision to Be Free.* Harper Collins Publishers. 1995.

Fox, Matthew. *Hildegard of Bingen: A Saint for Our Times. Unleashing Her Power in the 21st Century.* Namaste Publishing, Vancouver, Canada, 2012.

Fox, Matthew. *Illuminations of Hildegard of Bingen.* Text by Hildegard of Bingen with commentary by Matthew Fox. Bear and Company, Rochester, Vermont. 1985, 2002.

Furlong, Monica. *Visions and Longings: Medieval Women Mystics.* Shambala, Boston, 1997.

Grabhorn, Lynn. *Excuse Me, Your Life is Waiting: The Astonishing Power of Feelings.* Hampton Roads Publishing Company, Inc. 2000.

Hildegard of Bingen. *The Book of the Rewards of Life.* Translated by Bruce W. Hozeski. Oxford University Press, New York, Oxford. 1994.

Hildegard of Bingen's Book of Divine Works with Letters and Songs. Edited and Introduced by Matthew Fox. Bear and Company, Santa Fe, New Mexico. 1987.

Hildegard of Bingen. *Scivias.* Translated by Mother Columba Hart and Jane Bishop. Introduced by Barbara J. Newman. Preface by Caroline Walker Bynum. Paulist Press, New York. 1990.

Keating, Thomas. *Open Mind, Open Heart: The Contemplative Dimension of the Gospel.* Amity House, Amity, New York. 1986.

Levoy, Gregg. *Callings: Finding and Following an Authentic Life.* Three Rivers Press, New York. 1997.

Meninger, William, OCSO. *1012 Monastery Road: A Spiritual Journey.* Lantern Books, New York, a Division of Booklight, Inc. 2005.

Merton, Thomas. *New Seeds of Contemplation.* A New Directions Book. 1961.

Riso, Don Richard and Russ Hudson. *The Wisdom of the Enneagram: The Complete Guide for Psychological and Spiritual Growth for the Nine Personality Types.* Bantam Books. New York, Toronto, London, Sydney, Auckland. 1999.

Rohr, Richard. *Falling Upward: A Spirituality for the Two Halves of Life.* Jossey-Bass, a Wiley Imprint. www.josseybass.com. 2011.

Rohr, Richard. *The Naked Now: Learning to See as the Mystics See.* A Crossroad Book. The Crossroad Publishing Company, New York. 2009, 2013.

Sharratt, Mary. *Illuminations: A Novel of Hildegard of Bingen.* Mariner Books, Houghton Mifflin Harcourt, Boston, New York. 2012.

Teresa of Avila. *The Interior Castle.* Paulist Press. New York, Ramsey, Toronto. 1979.

Tolle, Eckhart. *The Power of Now.* New World Library, Novato, California. 1999.

About the Author

Author's photo by Anita Martinez

Catherine A. Engel taught elementary school music for thirty years in Kansas and Colorado. She taught all ages from kindergarten to adults and had a successful career as a clinician, teaching teachers how to teach. Ms. Engel also was active in Music Ministry in several different parishes, beginning at the age of seven when she started singing in the church choir alongside her mother, who encouraged her musical abilities. Although she always wrote songs and stories for her students, this is her first book.

74758351R00126

Made in the USA
Columbia, SC
16 September 2019